AN ORDINARY KIND *of* MIRACLE

Reflections on a faith-based community project in North Belfast

With grateful thanks
Bill

Philip Orr

Published by Philip Orr for the 174 Trust

ISBN 978-0-9568397-0-1

www.174trust.org

Designed by April Sky Design, Newtownards
028 9182 7195 www.aprilsky.co.uk

AN ORDINARY KIND *of* MIRACLE

Introduction

My first encounter with the 174 Trust was when I called into the Saltshaker on Belfast's lower Antrim Road, to grab a coffee and investigate this 'radical' new form of Christian outreach I had heard about. That was sometime in 1983, I seem to recall. Of course I wasn't to know it then, but fifteen years later I would begin a new phase of ministry as Director of the Trust.

By that stage the Trust had gone through a series of changes and been responsible for a whole range of activities and programs, delivered during violent and bloody times and affecting the lives of many people, some of whose stories are retold in the pages that follow.

Affecting lives, enabling people to make informed life choices and supporting them through often difficult periods, has been at the core of the Trust's ethos from the beginning. For the original visionaries and the many hundreds of volunteers who have carried the work forward, the words of Brenda Salter McNeil are an affirmation of their approach and commitment:

'The message of salvation is more than our verbal proclamation of the gospel. We must redefine evangelism to include how we live and interact with people - what it means for us to call them into God's family to become members of God's household. This is as important as our ability to accurately quote scriptures.'

- Brenda Salter McNeill, *A Credible Witness: Reflections on Power, Evangelism and Race*,(2008)

This volume recognizes and celebrates the efforts of so many people who, for more than a quarter of century, have sought to *be* 'good news' and in so doing, have made their own unique contribution towards the creation of a peaceful, tolerant and inclusive society.

Rev. Bill Shaw

1

BEGINNINGS

Beneath Cave Hill

The New Lodge area of North Belfast was ravaged by the conflict which plagued Northern Ireland from 1969 until the mid-1990s. It was a place where health was poor, unemployment was high, violent death was a regular occurrence and the inhabitants needed much courage in order to survive.

Violence and tension have not wholly gone away. North Belfast possesses many 'interfaces' where Protestant and Catholic communities exist side by side. Most local Protestants perceive themselves as beleaguered Unionist citizens of the United Kingdom whilst most local Catholics proclaim their Nationalism and their hunger for unity with the Irish Republic.

However huge changes have taken place in North Belfast throughout its history. In the 19th century, the lower Antrim Road was a fashionable place on the edge of a growing industrial town. Fine houses were built for wealthy owners, with gardens and orchards to match, in an era when Belfast was becoming an industrial powerhouse of the Empire. The houses were situated beneath the slopes of Cavehill, whose cliff-face towered over the waters of Belfast Lough.

The population of the lower Antrim Road during the 19th century was largely though not entirely Protestant. Neighbours in such fine houses would have been freed by material comfort and social success from the intense political colouring of the densely populated working-class communities which were evolving nearby. In these communities, men and women who had recently arrived from the countryside settled within specific areas where they could share secure, time-honoured cultural and religious allegiances. They lived in crowded streets, doing laborious jobs in the factories, mills and docks. One such area was the New Lodge. 'Mixed marriages' in the New Lodge were not uncommon and several Protestant families existed there but the vicinity had an identity which was Catholic and Nationalist in colouring. [1]

The Antrim Road had a number of imposing Protestant steeples. Not least of the ecclesiastical buildings was Duncairn Presbyterian Church, built in 1862. Some of the values of this congregation can be seen in the life of one member, Thomas Sinclair, who was a key figure in Belfast during the dynamic years before the Great War. He was a man of religious convictions who looked back to the Ulster Evangelical Revival of 1859 with devotion. Sinclair was committed to politics and was an architect of the Ulster Covenant, a document that was the focus of a campaign in 1912 to oppose the establishment of a new Irish parliament in Dublin. This campaign mobilised Protestant mass-support in the northern province of Ulster for the retention of undiluted union with Britain. It gained virtually no support from New Lodge Catholics, who aspired towards Irish autonomy and their own empowerment.[2]

In the early 1920s, Irishmen and women found themselves caught up in a conflict in which the newly-formed Irish Republican Army fought a guerrilla war against the forces of the British Crown. Republicans had won the majority of votes in Ireland in the election of 1918 and were incensed that Britain had not recognised this as a mandate for independence. Civil strife convulsed Belfast and other parts of the island. Unionists continued to stand firm on the claim to remain fully British. The boundary between the New Lodge and the nearby Tiger's Bay became one of many hotbeds of tension.[3]

The British government decided on a division of the island in 1921 into an independent southern Irish state where Catholics dominated and a British northern state with a Protestant majority. The latter entity comprised much of the territory of the ancient province of Ulster.

Belfast was torn by riots, assassinations and gun-battles. Then an uneasy calm settled on the newly partitioned island. Civil unrest was kept at bay in Northern Ireland, with only a few interruptions, for over forty years but in due course the Nationalists' sense of deep-seated grievance would come to the surface.

Lying in the dark with a Provo company

Belfast also experienced social change throughout the 20th century, in a way that characterises many urban environments. Throughout the latter decades of the 20th century, more of the middle-class inhabitants of the Antrim Road moved to suburban areas. Working-class people from the New Lodge who had managed to achieve upward mobility also moved. Architectural modernity arrived as several 'high-rise' blocks of flats were built for local residents in the 1960's, in an area known as The Barrack because of an earlier military depot on the site.

Many families still lived in the shadow of these towers, on North Belfast's red-brick terraced streets. They inhabited cramped houses with few amenities but those who lived there testify to a strong community spirit.[4] Then, in the late 1960s, a public campaign began for civil rights for the Catholic community in the north, inspired by human rights activists such as Martin Luther King in America. The campaign was seen by many inside the Protestant community as motivated by a desire to undermine the northern state. Northern Ireland re-entered a period of turmoil.

Soon, violence dominated everyday life in Belfast. In working-class Catholic parts of the city, the newly re-armed Irish Republican Army soon had strong support. Ulster's armed police-force was a very unwelcome presence in such places, especially when supplemented by units of the British Army. In working-class Protestant areas such as Tiger's Bay and the Lower Shankill, which lay close to the New Lodge, new Loyalist militias sprang up, aiming to fight a war against those members of adjacent communities who seemed bent on dismantling the union with Britain and destroying their heritage. Soon, much of North Belfast was deeply afflicted by 'ghettoisation'.

By the mid-1970s, the New Lodge area, including the formerly affluent lower Antrim Road, had become deeply Republican, although many New Lodge people can still point to Protestants who stayed on in comparative safety throughout the 'Troubles'. The Provisional Irish Republican Army possessed numerous volunteers in the area, armed with the ubiquitous 'Armalite' rifle. Their Marxist fellow-travellers, the Official I.R.A., split when that organisation declared a ceasefire in 1972. Their more militant wing, the Irish National Liberation Army. gained support in parts of the New Lodge.[5]

Protestant congregations such as Duncairn Presbyterian Church and Antrim Road Baptist Church were now standing in, or close to, what felt like an alien terrain. The Republican songs heard in the area chilled many Protestant church members, especially those with connections to the police or links to the Protestant fraternal body known as the Orange Order:

> 'And it's down in the New Lodge, that's where I long to be,
> Lying in the dark with a Provo company,
> A comrade on me left and another on me right,
> And a clip of ammunition for me little Armalite.'[6]

By the early 1980s, the death in prison of Republican hunger-strikers, led by Bobby Sands, involved even greater tensions in the New Lodge. These prisoners were protesting against the recent 'criminalisation' of the IRA and INLA campaigns through a punitive penal regime. As far as Republicans were concerned, these men were prisoners of war and not criminals. In the volatile hunger-strike era, there were thousands of soldiers and police on duty yet the violence intensified as the British government stood firm against penal reform and ten young Republican prisoners died before the protest came to an end.[7]

How could depleted Protestant churches survive in this district? How could they relate to local people and cross the religious fault-lines which had bedevilled Irish history without stirring up antagonism? Would church members not be in grave personal danger in the New Lodge? In the aftermath of Bobby Sands' death, a Protestant milkman and his son had died not far from the Duncairn church when their vehicle was stoned by rioters, impelled into street-violence by the news from Long Kesh gaol.[8]

And how would these churches tackle the issue of social class? The working-class inhabitants of Belfast's inner-city communities lived daily lives that were often marked by a deprivation unknown in the suburbs.

Star of the Sea

In actual fact, both the Duncairn Presbyterians and the Antrim Road Baptists had already struggled with communal tensions and been involved in trying to build bridges during the early years of the 'Troubles'.

Dermott McMullan had come to the Duncairn church in 1958 in a time of relative peace and calm and stayed until 1976. The big city church which he now occupied looked like a mini-cathedral, after his previous pastorate in the small rural parish of Portglenone. The Victorian manse at Duncairn had an open fireplace in almost every room and the bay window of his study offered a view of the Antrim Hills. In its window-seat, Mrs Piper, the wife of a previous incumbent, had been known to sit while doing her needlework.

When Dermott first arrived in North Belfast, nearly 200 Protestant families lived locally. On one occasion, 400 men connected to the nearby outreach project known as the Duncairn Mission gathered in the spacious garden at the back of the manse for a social event. Of course there were hints, during those pre-Troubles days, of underlying animosities. On the occasion of a British royal visit to the city, the caretaker at Duncairn draped a Union Jack along the railings at the front of the church. Dermott recalls the quiet comment made by one local Catholic man – 'There will be a day coming when you won't put that flag up...'

The minister of Duncairn noticed rising tensions in the late 1960s when football matches were played at a nearby stadium. Groups of supporters - divided by religion and team-loyalty - threw missiles at one another. When the conflict began 'in earnest' in 1969 and 1970, clashes between local youths and the security forces became regular features of life. In one week, more than 100 local Presbyterian families departed from the New Lodge, most leaving for brand-new houses in Ballygomartin in the Greater Shankill area. If a family wanted to move, all they had to do was present a letter of support from their clergyman to the City Council. With sadness, the minister of Duncairn penned these letters.

In the early riots, water-cannon and CS gas were used as crowd-control measures. Dermott was glad that in the manse there was always at least one room where the gas could not penetrate. On one occasion, when a thick cloud of gas was released, the church hall was opened so that people who had been caught up in a melee could come inside and recover. The Thomas Sinclair Hall, named after a hero of Unionism, had become a first-aid station for local Nationalists.

Walking around the church grounds afterwards, Dermott picked up several pounds' worth of loose change which had spilled from the pockets of local people who had pulled out their handkerchiefs to protect their faces from the fumes.

He placed the money in the box belonging to the church's benevolent fund.

As the 'Troubles' worsened, Dermott would turn on the radio, first thing in the morning, to hear the local news bulletins and find out where a bomb had gone off. One morning, he tuned in to find that a close relative had been shot in the Short Strand area of East Belfast, while on duty as a policeman.

However the rituals of church life at Duncairn had to go on, including weddings, funerals and christenings. Dermott recalls one incident where the wedding party was instructed by the nervous mother of the bride to make an exit via the side door onto Duncairn Gardens and 'not to hang about', lest they get caught up in an 'incident'.

During their time spent on the Lower Antrim Road, the McMorrans looked after Dermott's mother-in-law who was physically handicapped. When asked by the army to evacuate the Duncairn manse because of a bomb that was about to explode nearby, Dermott explained that his mother-in-law was immobile. The family members were allowed to stay on in the building, with the thick wooden shutters on the windows closed and barred. This bomb caused little damage. Other explosions brought structural damage to their church, including one device which went off nearby and in the process destroyed the premises of one of Belfast's antiquarian booksellers.

But good relations were maintained with local people. One day, children from the Catholic 'Star of the Sea' primary school were making their way up the Antrim Road when they got caught in a gun-battle between the army and the IRA. Dermott ushered the group into the church hall. There was a piano and so one of the teachers started to play traditional tunes and before long the children were performing Irish dances while the gunfire raged. Then Dermott gave the all-clear and the children returned to their classrooms on the other side of the Antrim Road.

Later he received a glass vase as a present for looking after the children. It was not the only gift Dermott and his family received. He still treasures the cut-glass ornaments presented to him by an Irish dance teacher who used a wooden hall belonging to the church, which was subsequently burned down.

Dermott McMorran gained respect for his work with the Belfast education authorities. He sat on the governmental boards of several Catholic schools in the city. When he spoke at a school assembly in St Patrick's Catholic Secondary School on the Antrim Road, this proved to be of great benefit to community relations as he was recognised from now on as a man with a role inside their educational sector.

However , on one occasion a Catholic priest was killed in the city and a member of the British Army called with Dermott to warn him to be 'on the look-out'. The security forces felt there was a real danger that Dermott might become the victim of yet another 'tit-for-tat' killing.

Despite his efforts at maintaining good relations and staunching the flow of Protestants out of the New Lodge, Dermott witnessed an inexorable decline in his congregation. Probably a third of the church members left during his tenure. Very many others retained membership but moved to the suburbs. Amongst those who beat a hasty retreat were the prison warders who had worked in Crumlin Road gaol and had lived in special housing in Girdwood Park.

Prison officers became IRA targets when Nationalists underwent incarceration.

Added to the decline in church membership were the incidents in which young lives were lost. One of the darkest moments was when a police officer whose family belonged to the church was shot in Londonderry. His funeral service took place at Duncairn, on a day when the security forces saturated the area with troops, due to the presence of so many high profile policemen and politicians at the ceremony. On another occasion, when driving through the streets on his way to take a Sunday evening service, Dermott saw the bodies of two young British soldiers lying on the street. They had become victims of IRA sniper fire. Leading the worship that night was far from easy.[9]

Do you ever read the Bible?

The Baptist church on the Antrim Road had had a long tradition of practical concern for the community, as first evidenced by a small schoolroom erected beside the main premises, when the church was built, back in 1897.

Roy McMullan came to the pastorate in 1967. His congregation included several people who were living in the very heart of the New Lodge, in locations such as Spamount Street and Upper Meadow Street.

Like Dermott McMorran, Roy stayed on in the 'thick of things' as the 'Troubles' erupted. He lived in a manse next door to the church and he brushed up glass from his broken window-panes alongside his Catholic neighbours when they were all affected by bomb-blasts. He worried about his children who attended a nursery school on the New Lodge Road. His wife was involved with the school and got to know the principal, who encouraged the establishment of a cross-community play-group on the church premises in 1972, a group that was the ancestor of a project that still exists today.

Roy made efforts to connect with Catholic clergy, who in turn appeared at Baptist prayer-meetings. He helped to host public discussions where Baptist and Catholic clergy talked about their faith traditions, trying to replace ignorance and suspicion with accurate knowledge. Roy encouraged Catholic parents to send their children to youth events in the church, stressing that they faced no threat. In 1971, massive civil disruption followed the arrest and internment of men and women whom the Northern Ireland government considered to be Republican 'suspects.' Half a dozen Catholic families bedded down in the church hall and manse because they could not get home.

Roy McMullan left in September 1972 to take up a post in the Irish Baptist College. In 1975, an Englishman named Trevor Brock succeeded Roy. Trevor tried to keep moving the church away from nostalgia for its more comfortable past and towards greater interaction with the locals. The play-group grew and 70% of those who came to it were from a Catholic background, glad of facilities to ease the burdens of parenthood in an area of few resources. At a later stage, the numbers fell because other play-group provision was established in the neighbourhood. By the late 1970s, the church's Girls' Brigade Company was dominantly Catholic. Many parents felt it was an organisation that took their children off the dangerous North Belfast streets and engaged them in positive activities.

Trevor recalls that most young people who came into his church, either from the New Lodge or nearby Catholic areas, were well-behaved. He recalls few sectarian issues emerging during youth work although the building suffered overnight arson attacks and vandalism from some disaffected locals. However this brought Catholic parents to the doors of the church to ask if they could help repair the damage. But one unpleasant occasion does stand out in the mind of Baptist church-goers. Once, during the sermon, they witnessed lumps of coal hurtling through a window, adjacent to the choir.

However Trevor and his congregation knew they must continue to make their presence felt despite any threat of vandalism. They manned a bookstall each Saturday morning, across the road from the church. It was a means of interacting with local people.[10]

In 1977, a Presbyterian minister called Patton Taylor arrived on the Antrim Road as the pastor of Duncairn Church. He was originally from Scotland but had already spent some years in ministry in Ireland. At his inauguration, a number of Catholic neighbours from Thorndale Avenue were in attendance at the service, in an expression of goodwill which made an impact upon the Scotsman.

Baptist leaders recognised that joint activity with Duncairn was a sensible sharing of resources, especially as Patton was an advocate of community involvement. A combined summer scheme for young people seemed a good idea as July and August were months when children were not at school. They were at risk of involvement in the trouble which flared on the streets.[11]

Ricky Allen grew up in Thorndale Avenue and was soon aware of the new project. He was four years old in 1977, when a tall thin Scotsman with ginger hair knocked on all the doors in his street, to invite the children to the Duncairn summer scheme. Ricky recalls boyhood visits to the arts and crafts sessions where he made colourful book-marks with Scripture texts inscribed upon them.

He recollects the childlike wonder with which he entered the spacious church hall, where children were allowed to 'let off steam' to their heart's content. He remembers the enchanted space of Patton's garden, tucked in behind the manse, where barbeques were enjoyed in summer weather.[12]

Despite the problems that could have been posed by two rather dark, somewhat forbidding and very Protestant buildings, these summer schemes worked well in the New Lodge and kept on evolving until the 1990s. Clubs for juniors took place in the morning and afternoon. Then in the evenings, an informal coffee-bar was created to attract teenagers, who were invited to come to 'follow-up' studies, where the benefits of a living Christian faith could be explored. [13]

Sometimes, if the scene was quiet, these volunteer workers ventured onto the Antrim Road or into the Waterworks Park to meet young people with invites or questionnaires, including questions such as 'Do you believe in God?' and 'Do you ever read the Bible?' Trevor stresses that local people saw the summer schemes bring occupation and mentoring to North Belfast's Catholic youngsters, some of whom had had a parent who was serving a sentence in gaol or who had been interned.

Trevor left the Antrim Road in 1980 for another pastorate. By this time Patton Taylor was planning outreach that would last 'all year round.' He wanted a scheme that addressed the economic and social needs of the district.

Of course, Trevor and Patton had found some scepticism among their congregations about youth outreach projects, as these did not employ the very direct preaching that was obligatory in local Evangelical tradition, during which the message of personal conversion, followed by enrolment in the ranks of a 'sound' Protestant church, was enthusiastically and explicitly extolled. This 'new gospel' seemed to go too gently on the 'conversion' message and mention nothing about the 'Biblical' basis of Protestantism. Its practitioners talked too much about meeting social needs and dealing with community problems, rather than focusing only on 'affairs of the soul'.

Trevor also says:

'I see the difficulties my congregation faced. We were not going to build a solid church by doing youth work with Catholic kids in the summer and chatting to a few local lads on a Saturday night. But I felt the kids we worked with should be helped, both socially and spiritually. And they were not all "damaged goods". I had seen more threatening behaviour from teenagers carrying knives in a part of Scotland where I'd worked. '

He was heartened to see young people in his congregation take on responsibility. One such person was Sharon Frizell whose father owned a fish shop on the Shankill Road. Trevor baptised Sharon on profession of her faith before he left. She had a 'heart' for young people and built friendships with Catholic teenagers, some of whom attended the Baptist youth club which followed up the summer schemes on a weekly basis.[14]

The Good News Club

By the third year of the summer scheme, Patton drew in volunteers from Ireland, England and the USA. He also involved Henry Berry, a worker with the Child Evangelism Fellowship. Henry was still working for the CEF when interviewed in 2009. He describes the CEF as 'an international, interdenominational and evangelical organisation whose primary goals are to evangelise unsaved children and edify Christian children.' Henry and Patton became very good friends. Henry founded the 'Good News Club' which met in Duncairn on Wednesday nights. He was also responsible for the children's outreach, every summer. The programme included enjoyable and active games such as 'Port and Starboard' and 'Cat and Mouse'. When energy had been expended, the children met in the Church Hall for their 'Bible Time', which consisted of singing choruses, learning Bible verses, taking part in a quiz and listening to a Bible lesson. One series of talks was based on the colours of the famous 'Wordless Book.'

In this book, as Henry explains:

'the gold page stood for Heaven, the dark page represented sin, the red page reminded everyone of Christ's love and death on the cross of Calvary and the white page spoke of the great doctrine of justification. The outer green page reminded the children who trusted in the Lord Jesus as their Saviour about the importance of Christian growth.'

Henry believes that this programme was conducted in a very 'scriptural' and 'sensitive' way. At no stage was there any dramatic 'appeal' made for converts but, nonetheless:

'much prayer was offered to God that He would work in the lives of the children.'

At the end of each meeting, the children received orange juice and biscuits and then did some handcrafts.

The songs were a favourite with everybody. One was a short chorus that gave the children's club its title:

> 'Good news, good news, Christ died for me,
> Good news, good news, if I believe,
> Good news, good news, I'm saved eternally,
> That's wonderful extra good news...'

Scripture verses were also committed to memory, such as Romans chapter 5 verse 8, which focuses on love and redemption:

'God commends His love to us in that while we were yet sinners, Christ died for us.'

The logistics of the outing at the end of the holiday club were always a challenge. On one occasion, visiting the Ulster Transport Museum, Henry discovered a couple of the children perched on top of a historic exhibit and he had to coax them down.

He found support among the parents for the Good News Club and was always transparent with them, placing his contact details on the literature and inviting them to come to the meetings to see what was going on. He felt that the parents were very happy with what was taking place. On one occasion three children from the area attended the Good News Club camp which he conducted in the CEF holiday centre in Kilkeel. They returned to the New Lodge and shared their experience with many friends.

In the following year, there were so many children from the Duncairn area wanting to attend the camp that Henry had to organise one holiday solely for them. This practice continued for a number of years. The programme at the camp consisted of a 'Bible Time', and a medley of sports, handcrafts, swimming and outings to Tollymore Forest Park or local beaches or the seaside resort of Newcastle.

Henry also participated in the work with teenagers, which was led by his friend Philip Campbell. In looking back, he says he found this work both a 'blessing' and a 'challenge'. He believes that the team members needed much 'God-given wisdom' in answering direct questions which the teenagers asked and in dealing with tense situations, brought on by the drug or alcohol addictions that were beginning to affect too many young people in the area .

Henry was involved in his work in the New Lodge for seven years and feels 'very grateful to the Lord' that Patton ever asked him to be involved. Henry met with the other workers, each Tuesday morning in the Duncairn manse where Patton resided, in order to pray for the young people of the area.

The breakfasts which Henry Berry describes usually began at 7a.m. but that did not deter keen summer-time volunteers from coming to the New Lodge on a regular basis throughout the winter, such as university student Mary Malanaphy who travelled several miles from Carrickfergus by train.[15]

However, Patton recalls one occasion in the early 1980s when he knew he must re-imagine the whole process of interaction with Catholic North Belfast.:

'It had been a long night. The coffee-bar outreach of the previous evening had gone well enough. The music group had been given a good hearing. Round the tables the young people were asking penetrating questions. There was a real searching for spiritual reality. However an uneasy air of tension hung over the hall. That evening there was an uneasy stand-off between the angry young men on the streets and the nervous police and army patrols. Suddenly the door of the hall burst open. "The Brits are coming" someone shouted. Within moments the hall had emptied and a full-scale riot was under way in the Lower Antrim Road outside.'

However the team in the Duncairn Presbyterian church hall escaped unscathed that night as it usually did, and when they met the next morning a team member from North Belfast came up with a surprising observation:

"You've got it all wrong" she said "You think that the barriers between you and these kids are because of politics and because of the Protestant-Catholic thing. But the real barrier between you and the kids is that you're all so middle-class and affluent. You come in from outside and you don't know what it's like to live around here."

At moments like this, Patton believed the work in the area could only be furthered by a project that brought a team of committed helpers into the local community to live, work and share their lives - with all the 'culture-shock' and personal risk that might entail.[16]

Throughout the next few months, he set about raising money for the purchase of premises adjacent to his church, situated at 174 Antrim Road near the junction between the main thoroughfare and the New Lodge Road. The transaction was completed by 1983, with the bulk of finance provided by well-disposed Christian businessmen who had been convinced of the innovative nature of this project and its peace-making potential. Property prices in the New Lodge had been greatly depressed by the 'Troubles' and this made the transaction more feasible.

The property which had been acquired was a large house that had seen better days. It had been built when this part of the city had a genteel air. Now it consisted of two bare commercial areas on the ground floor, above which were three flats, including one which was basically an attic space.

The committee which Patton set up to supervise the project decided that a cafe should be created in the downstairs area. It would be named the 'Saltshaker' to indicate the 'salt and light' spoken of by Jesus, as emblems of a spiritual presence in the world. Space would also be available for recreation, including a coffee bar in the evenings. An organisation known as the '174 Trust' was set up. It had charitable status, and it used a symbol that possessed a rich array of interlocked meanings.

The numbers 1, 7 and 4 overlapped to form two crosses. This denoted the cross-roads where the Antrim Road met the New Lodge Road. It presented Christ's cross at the centre of the project. The cross also represented suffering and deprivation and it hinted at 'crossing over' the gulf of Northern Ireland's sectarian divide.

Patton hoped that the volunteers who worked at 174 would plan to live in the area, whether in the flats above the Saltshaker or in other premises nearby. Plans were afoot for creating a local branch of the government's Action for Community Employment (ACE) scheme which subsidised short-term work projects amidst the severe job-losses and economic recession of the early 1980's. There would soon be a mums' and toddlers' group, a youth club and a pensioners' organisation at the trust. The 'Saltshaker' community cafe soon began to operate. All these projects would offer help to an area where the social infrastructure had been devastated by the conflict. A director of the trust would soon be installed, who would live above the cafe and undertake to be 'on call' at all times.[17]

2

THE SALTSHAKER YEARS

In The Shadow Of The Watch-Tower

The first director was Mary Malanaphy, who had been raised in a Catholic family in rural County Fermanagh, not far from the Irish border. While studying at the University of Ulster, she embarked on a faith journey that brought her into contact with the college's Christian Union, an organisation whose members in Northern Ireland were very largely from a Protestant background. It was a perceived switch of allegiance that led to disapproval amongst her family. But although Mary went on to express her faith by undergoing adult baptism in a Protestant church in Carrickfergus, she believed she was now neither 'Protestant' nor 'Catholic' but simply 'a follower of Christ.'

This new if controversial commitment had energised Mary to volunteer during her summer vacations for work at 174. Then, having completed her Masters' Degree at the University of Ulster, she applied for the 174 directorship and gained the post. She moved into the flat above the Saltshaker cafe. And so she began the formidable task of making this visionary project work. The 174's management, made up of members of the Presbyterian and Baptist churches, hoped she would be helped by her Catholic background to forge strong links with the New Lodge community.[18]

Other young volunteers began to assemble around her, many of whom were from more 'orthodox' Ulster Protestant backgrounds. One was Heather Johnston, who had been brought up in a farming family in County Tyrone. She was a close acquaintance of Mary's at university. Shortly after Mary's appointment, Heather moved into the flat with her friend. Working for the civil service through the day, Heather led the 174 Trust's activities in the evenings. She was joined each night by a few other volunteers, all of whom received training from the experienced youth worker, Maurice Kinkead.

Heather and Mary found the 174 premises primitive. Water seeped through a hole in the roof when it rained and the atmosphere was dank and cold. Given her tranquil rural background, it was a surreal and scary experience for Heather to sit at night in a flat overlooking the dark thoroughfare of the Antrim Road. She had received recent advice to 'mind the snipers', which added to her trepidation.[19]

The other flats on the premises were at first rented out to local people, in an endeavour to break down barriers between 174 and the New Lodge community. Heather made contact with a young woman who walked with an obvious limp. On enquiring about her disability, Heather was matter-of-factly informed that this was due to a wound caused when her Armalite rifle had gone off accidentally during 'active service' with the IRA.

At night, as Heather prepared for bed and the local pubs shut, she watched the New Lodge men stop in the shadow of a watchtower belonging to the British Army and shout abuse at the soldiers who were manning it. If times were quiet, verbal banter and barbed jokes were exchanged but if there had been a recent 'incident' in the district, the exchanges involved a hail of missiles, hurled at the inmates of the tower.[20] During the years of its existence, that watchtower came under rocket attack no less than fourteen times.[21]

Heather discovered that many university friends with Protestant backgrounds would not visit her on the Antrim Road. There was fear of being located, even for a few daylight hours, within a Nationalist area. They felt they might be suspected of espionage or membership of the security forces. However, a few Protestant acquaintances did in fact make their way to the Saltshaker flat to visit the volunteers.

Heather's background was not filled with anti-Catholic attitudes that outsiders have often presumed to be completely typical of Ulster Protestants. Indeed her Baptist mother looked after a vulnerable Catholic neighbour and brought the lady into her home to care for her. Heather had been used to friendly, relaxed relationships between members of 'the two communities', including regular appearances in her house of the local priest, who came to administer the sacraments to the Catholic woman.

Supplementing this, Heather's friendship with Mary Malanaphy had enabled her to see that a lot of Catholics hungered for real experiences of faith, just as she did, and that they were not the benighted slaves to 'Romanism' that some Protestant clerics had described over many decades. Thus Heather was prepared for the cultural exchanges of the 174 Trust, in a manner that many young people in her peer-group were not.

Mary and Heather look back in wonder at the naive enthusiasm with which they tackled the youth work at the trust. On the first night, a heater disappeared and a large stereo 'music-machine' vanished, both stolen by boys who had taken the objects to the rear of the premises and out of a back door that the 174 leaders had not yet discovered. After an intense appeal to their audience about 'trust' and 'responsibility', on the following night the music-machine was returned. A major problem was the unacceptability of calling the police when such 'crimes' were committed.[22]

One young woman who volunteered at 174 was Lois Balmer, who lived in a suburban area of the city, further along the Antrim Road, and whose parents were members of the Baptist Church. She had been a volunteer on youth-teams which went each summer to Baptist churches in the Irish Republic. So she had gained some awareness of 'Catholic Ireland.' However the New Lodge, on her own doorstep, was a more daunting proposition.

She found the vicinity volatile. She often watched it explode into violence, directed at the security forces. Seeing petrol bombs explode on the street outside the Saltshaker was a new experience. She was also conscious of her own inexperience. After all, she was only a few years older than the young people she was supervising in the youth club.

Heather, Lois and Mary were delighted when an art project got under way. Mary's boyfriend, Johnny, was an art student and he had a friend who decided to paint a mural for the bare interior walls of the building. The first stage of the project involved the teenagers. They sketched their ideas for what should go into the mural. However the drawings were an amazing sight. The dominant image was of weaponry, drawn with loving and knowledgeable attention to detail. Eventually the gun motif was replaced by something more suitable for a 'Christian cafe'. The final version of the mural portrayed a row of shop-fronts along the lower Antrim Road, including an endearing depiction of the Saltshaker, which showed Mary Malanaphy looking benignly across the New Lodge through her window in the upstairs flat.[23]

Among the young men who started to use the Saltshaker on a regular basis was Joe McGuigan. Just prior to its opening, Joe and his friends had been approached on the street by a couple of 174 volunteers who proffered them leaflets that advertised a new youth club located at 174 Antrim Road.

So on the first night, a bunch of boys were gathered at the door, waiting for it to open. After all there was nothing for them to do in the New Lodge, unless they went to Duncairn Gardens and waited for a crowd to gather on either side of the road. They would throw stones and bottles at one another and exchange loud taunts.

Soon Joe was a regular at the trust, revelling in the safe and warm environment of the 'back room'. Some of his fondest memories from those Saltshaker nights are of the 'movie evenings' held in the 'back room', when popular films were shown on a 'video player'. He also recalls a 24 hour pool-playing marathon, which was organised to raise money for charity. Soon there were weekend camping trips, organised and staffed by the 174 youth leaders.

Joe was fond of drawing and he was soon recruited to provide a few pictures for the walls, including pencil sketches of the Saltshaker regulars. He took special pride in a portrait of his hero, the Jamaican reggae star Bob Marley. A 174 volunteer called Marty Quaile possessed qualifications as a mechanic and he offered Joe and his friends the chance to learn useful skills that would stand them in good stead when applying for a job.

Joe availed of the ACE scheme. He began to develop the painting and decorating skills from which he went on to make a living. Besides all this, the cafe at the trust was soon a second home to him. Nothing was more welcome than the tasty, filling food which was served there. One of the popular items was a jacket potato, smothered in grated cheese.[24]

Off the streets, where danger lurked

Another young woman involved in running the 174 Trust was Laura Coulter. Her background was one of relative comfort as a middle-class East Belfast Protestant who had attended an all-girls' grammar school set in pleasant surroundings. However a spell in Sierra Leone - when her father moved to Africa to work - had broadened Laura's girlhood horizons. Then as an 18 year old she spent time in the city of Cork in the Irish Republic, working for the evangelistic organisation called Campus Crusade. This was a formative experience as she had an opportunity to encounter an Irish culture that made few appearances in East Belfast. She enjoyed going to ceilidhs and participating in Irish dancing.

Then Laura went to university and met her future husband, after which she gained valuable experience as a volunteer at the Christian Renewal Centre in Rostrevor, County Down. Subsequently she worked at the Belfast YMCA, having undertaken a catering course which enabled her to run their cafe. The centre was one of those healing spaces where Christians from both sides of the societal divide would meet, talk and worship. Laura was thus equipped to handle some of the challenges of interaction with the Catholic (or post-Catholic) people of the New Lodge. She replied to an advertisement for someone to run the cafe at the Saltshaker and she was offered the job.

Looking back at those early days in the trust, Laura feels that nothing prepared her for the shock of travelling to the lower Antrim Road. The trust existed in the shadow of the huge watchtower which was used for round-the-clock surveillance by the garrison in the nearby Girdwood Barracks. At nights, as Heather Johnston had discovered, that watchtower was often a target of abuse. Squads of soldiers emerged from the barracks gates each day, to patrol the streets with loaded guns.

Laura did not live 'on the premises' but she had a huge role to play as the cafe supervisor, preparing lunches from fresh products every day and organising a team of local helpers who had been recruited through the ACE scheme.

Pensioners from the district and young lads like Joe McGuigan were the main customers at the cafe. And as in any inner-city area, with its considerable quota of loneliness and poverty, people came in for company, shelter and inexpensive food. As well as providing the food, Laura had to keep a close eye on 174's resources. The contents of the freezer went missing on one occasion and a television vanished. The latter incident prompted Laura's deputy – a young man recruited from the neighbourhood – to suggest they should send for the local 'heavies' to 'sort out' those who were strongly suspected of organising the theft.

She had eight ACE employees in her team at the cafe. A number of other young people were based at the premises, engaged in an ACE-funded range of painting, maintenance and decorating activities in the New Lodge. Laura was less likely to be there in the evening, when the back room on the ground floor functioned as a 'drop-in' centre. But she knew the centre kept some youngsters off the streets where danger lurked.

Laura will never forget the violence that be-devilled inner-city Belfast in the 1980s. Buses were hijacked and set alight on the Antrim Road with frightening regularity. Riots erupted. IRA men and soldiers shot at each other. For riot control, the troops used CS gas and plastic bullets. They sometimes amused themselves in quieter times by throwing improvised missiles at locals from their armoured vehicles as they drove past. Laura recalls 174 volunteers and their clients arriving into the cafe, spattered with paint or smashed eggs.

Stories of police raids on houses at six in the morning were narrated in the Saltshaker. Anger was expressed at how homes were left in a mess after a fruitless search for guns hidden under floorboards or in bedroom cupboards. Laura also knew boys who used the Saltshaker premises and who disappeared for several days at a time as they had been taken into police custody for sustained interrogation.

Meanwhile in the world beyond the lower Antrim Road, the conflict continued, involving Republican and Loyalist militias, the Royal Ulster Constabulary and the British Army. Many uninvolved civilians lost their lives as well as the 'combatants'.

Some young men who used the cafe joked with Laura that they were going to siphon off the fuel in her moped to make petrol bombs to fire at the security forces or to set shops alight. On one occasion, two men who had parked in a car outside the Saltshaker kept the cafe under baleful surveillance throughout the day and rumours went around the premises that the local unit of the IRA had at last decided that 'this place is going to burn.'

However no harm came to Laura or anyone she knew who worked for the trust. In fact she started to believe that the local Republican leadership was protecting 174 from danger, due to the help it was offering the community.[25] Laura's view is backed up by the reports of several former Saltshaker clients. They confirm that local lads were told by IRA leaders that the trust must not be touched.[26]

There were also ideological reasons for protecting the trust, which came from the Irish Republican theory that ordinary Protestants were not the foe but rather the British imperial infrastructure in Northern Ireland. Protestants must be 'won over' to a pluralist Irish identity that would emerge as Britain left.

However, the British presence included its representatives in the police, the judiciary, and other local branches of the 'establishment,' as well as those who gave them aid and succour – largely Ulster Protestants. So claims of non-sectarianism did not convince most Ulster Protestants or indeed many Ulster Catholics.

It should be noted that other Protestant premises in North Belfast did suffer grave damage due to attacks, even if the infant 174 Trust did not. Antrim Road Baptist church suffered two serious assaults during the tenure of Pastor Keith Gilbert. The second attack, in 1988, resulted in a badly damaged building that had to be vacated for a considerable period of time.

Despite such alarming events the 174 Trust's ACE project continued to flourish. At its height in the mid-to-late 1980's, there were over 80 people on the 174 payroll. It was the only real employer in this economically desolate area. The ACE bosses in central Belfast seemed glad to have the trust on their side as administrators in the New Lodge.

The presence of so many local people in ACE jobs at the premises was considered a plus by the Evangelical leaders of the trust. It offered a chance to witness to them about the value of a committed, Christian way of life. Early-morning prayers in the Saltshaker were open to all ACE workers if they wished to attend. Patton Taylor and his team hoped that local people would begin to see the positive realities of personal faith.[27]

Many people found that the ACE scheme brought them help in all kinds of practical ways, even if an Evangelical conversion did not occur. ACE was helping them to put a first step on the ladder that would raise them towards a more fulfilling and effective life. One such person was Mary Connolly, who had originally come from south-east Antrim to live in the area in 1983 and who found the 174 Trust to be a welcome resource. She valued the trust's nursery facilities, which were housed in the Duncairn church premises. Placing her child in this nursery, she signed on at 174 for a year's ACE funding in order to study for a qualification in childcare.

When that year ended, Mary obtained a permanent position as a qualified childcare worker in the Ligoniel Family Centre. She then undertook a university degree in 'early years' education and childcare. She became a significant figure in developing care and education for infants in the city – a provision recognised as crucial in addressing the educational and social deficit in many working-class areas.[28]

Tail end Charlie with a loaded rifle

Over the years, thousands of British soldiers served in the New Lodge and emerged on foot-patrol each day from Girdwood, past the Duncairn Presbyterian church, to patrol the vicinity. The primary duty of policing the area had long since fallen mainly into the hands of the soldiers.

The daily experience was terrifying for both soldiers and locals. To men of the Royal Marines, the IRA volunteers were known as the 'zapmen' and they were respected as combatants who could kill with one volley from an automatic M16 or the blast from a Rocket Propelled Grenade. As one Marine would later explain:

'if you made the boat back home with your body still in one piece and with all limbs in working order, then you'd had a successful tour of duty'.

Each tour lasted for several months and involved a series of exhausting patrols. Rumours went around the barracks that the lights in the windows of the New Lodge's high-rise flats were used to flash signals to IRA units about the location of army patrols. There was an ice-cream van whose tune was believed to act as a signal to the gunmen. Soldiers felt that every civilian standing on a street corner might just be on 'look-out' duty for the IRA. Anyone carrying a bulky object in a bag might be holding a 'coffee jar bomb' – an improvised grenade, containing shrapnel, explosives and a detonator which could kill within a radius of several yards.

The Marines' street patrols followed the usual pattern, with two men leading the troupe, their rifles poised. Six men walked in the middle and a 'tail-end Charlie' with a loaded rifle walked backwards at the rear.

Nearby, a Saracen armed vehicle was manned by an experienced driver. Walking down the streets, the soldiers kept their eyes open for derelict houses - potential booby-trap sites.

During night patrols, the Marines tried each door-handle for if the door was not locked, it might indicate that the house had been vacated and that an IRA ambush was about to be staged from the premises. By the time the troops arrived back to Girdwood, they were pumped full of adrenalin. Large measures of Bushmills whiskey were poured out to calm nerves and prepare men for sleep.[29]

The troops often acted in ways that aroused great anger in the New Lodge population. Reacting to rumours of an IRA unit in the area, the army would seal off streets and search houses one by one, placing that community under curfew and intruding into private spaces. Everyone was a 'suspect', whether they were 'involved' or not.[30]

During Joe McGuigan's childhood, his father had been critically injured by British Army gunfire. He had returned to his home from the pub one night in 1974 and had gone outside to relieve himself – an indoor toilet was only installed in many New Lodge households in the late 1970s. Shortly afterwards he fell back into the house, bleeding profusely, as his family watched in horror, then rushed to summon an ambulance. Soldiers of the Royal Marines burst into their home with loaded rifles. Joe looked up and observed one of the soldiers shaking. He presumes that that soldier was the one who wounded his dad.

With prompt medical care, his father survived.[31]

Such stories as this were often heard in the Saltshaker.

I felt abandoned by God

Tony Macaulay was a volunteer at the 174 Trust in the 1980s. He had grown up in the Greater Shankill area, which was famous for its Protestant working-class identity. The Shankill had fallen on hard times as industry collapsed in the city. Poverty was endemic as it was in the New Lodge. However, Loyalists on the Shankill did not feel much solidarity with North Belfast Catholics in similar circumstances to themselves. Republican combatants had attacked targets on the Shankill Road and Loyalists had assaulted the New Lodge with explosives and bullets.

Tony's associations with the Shankill could have been a source of danger when he chose to work at 174. However, while attending a grammar school just a short distance along the Antrim Road, he had developed a Christian faith and had already done his first stint of volunteering on the 174 summer scheme. So he was not unfamiliar with the New Lodge area, its dangers and challenges. The political sensibilities within his family helped Tony to come to terms with the left-wing Republican values he would discover in the New Lodge. His father had had Socialist leanings.

Tony came to the 174 Trust as a full-time worker in 1986. He recalls being motivated by a desire to share his faith with the local people. He moved into a flat above the Saltshaker and in the evenings he sat in the 'back room' behind the cafe, playing games with the 'clients', listening to music with them, drinking cups of coffee and trying to strike up conversations that would lead towards 'personal belief in Jesus Christ as Saviour and Lord'. [32]

Tony recalls one young man who came to the centre, whose name was Billy Kane. He lived in Upper Meadow Street. He played the flute and was committed to Republicanism. When Billy was a little boy, his father had died in a 'no-warning' bombing of the nearby McGurk's Bar, during 1971.[33] Tony remembers Billy speaking about his father's death and thought that Billy looked worn, unwell and tired.

Tony's partner Lesley was soon tied into the work of the trust, even though she was not employed there. Lesley began a job as a youth worker in the Highfield estate in the Greater Shankill, during the mid-1980s. In recognition of Patton Taylor's vision that 174 should have workers who lived close by, Tony and Lesley resided in a house in the area after their marriage in 1986. Lesley worked with young people who faced the same problems as the inhabitants of the New Lodge. However the young people of Highfield existed in isolation from teenage Nationalists.

Lesley did 'personal development work' with the Highfield group in a way that paralleled the activities at the Saltshaker. She took an interest in the lives of her youth club members and endeavoured to build their self-worth. Lesley's biography was not typical for a woman from an Ulster Protestant background. Growing up in the largely Catholic village of Bellaghy in southern County Derry, she had lived next door to the McGlinchey family, which included Dominic who was a very active Republican.[34]

Another volunteer at the Saltshaker was Dave Maley from Birmingham who had studied at Cambridge University. He responded to an advertisement in the 'Careforce' Christian volunteer magazine. Dave arrived in Belfast in 1987, hoping to be part of a vibrant Christian community on the front-line of the toughest urban environment on these islands. However he found his experiences of North Belfast disorienting and felt that his Oxbridge Christian Union faith was of little help in those first weeks:

'I felt utterly abandoned by God. Where was this God that my Bible, my peers and my pastors had promised would be with me wherever I went?'

Night after night, Dave was found in the 'back room' of the Saltshaker, playing pool, table tennis or darts with the New Lodge boys. Often there was a struggle to contain their behaviour. One night a 'customer' handcuffed himself to a pillar, to prevent himself from being 'thrown out' when the cafe was shut for the night.

Dave recalls the weekly 'Bible Clubs' and marvels that so many of the street-wise New Lodge lads were at ease attending them. On one occasion, when Dave sought to go around the district, handing out invitations to this club, he was relieved to receive help from Billy Kane. Billy felt that Dave – who possessed an obvious 'Brummy' accent – was vulnerable on his leafleting trip and could well be suspected of espionage. So the young man accompanied Dave on his 'missionary journey', to offer 'protection'.

Dave spent the next five years at 174, working with people such as Billy. He had had high-minded missionary ideals when he came from England. But soon he felt that the youth of the New Lodge offered him as much help as he was giving them. Sometimes this came across through simple incidents. Some 'lads' turned up at his flat one night, perturbed to find Dave on his own.

'Well, we are here to bring you a bit of company' they proclaimed.

They had initially 'taken the hand' out of Dave, who gave away his possessions to anyone who asked for them, whether that included money or shoes. Then they grew to respect this selflessness. They knew Dave was highly educated, unlike them. Then legendary stories went around about Dave reading his books by the light of burning buses at the Saltshaker window. Perhaps he was becoming 'one of their own.'

But the black, unpredictable nature of Belfast humour was unsettling. On one occasion, as an IRA funeral was going past the trust with a tricolour-covered coffin and a cortege of black taxis, a Saltshaker client who was well known to Dave looked up from the street and witnessed him peering from a window. He called out in jest:

'Look, it's a Brit spy!'

Fortunately, no-one in the Republican ranks reacted to this mock-accusation.

Although he saw few dramatic religious conversions, Dave feels that the worth of the enterprise and of his own endeavour should not be judged by this measure. He believes that the work done by his fellow-volunteers helped many young people reach for a better future. That journey would take some of them – at least temporarily - beyond the lower Antrim Road, which many of its young inhabitants had scarcely ever left.

Dave thinks of one young man who told him:

'If I stay in the New Lodge it will suck me down.'

At first Dave felt that the area must not lose lads like this. However this boy went on with Dave's eventual encouragement to study for a degree. The college was a couple of miles across the city yet in reality it was a vast distance away, beyond the experiential horizons of most young people in this part of North Belfast.[35]

Meanwhile, Ricky Allen had discovered the Saltshaker café, where the inimitable 'Roberta' held sway in the kitchen. Even with 10p in his pocket to pay his way, Ricky was not denied a slice of toast and a cup of tea. And as for the weekly youth club, Ricky wouldn't have missed it. Even at other times, he wandered up the 174 stairs to chat to the youth workers or spent a couple of hours 'hanging out' with them on the street outside the café.

Ricky recalls how on one occasion, in the aftermath of a riot, a car was burning on the road and Dave Maley, who was still new to the area, was standing on the footpath watching the flames. Ricky took up a position behind the tall Englishman so Dave asked:

'Why are you hiding like that?'

Ricky replied with a single word:

'Shrapnel!'.

Dave scarpered.

Ricky had known that a burning vehicle could explode when its petrol tank caught fire but Dave still possessed little awareness of that kind of danger.

Ricky had a sense that the volunteers at the trust were 'more privileged than us' as some of them had degrees and jobs and owned nice cars. Most of them spoke with a softer accent and seemed to have a gentler view of life. This made it all the more remarkable that they should spend time living and working in the New Lodge.

However, Ricky did come from 'Thorndale', a street that felt somewhat apart from the rest of the New Lodge. The houses were bigger. People often owned vehicles. There was a more relaxed approach to the presence of the army and young Ricky had even chatted to soldiers and asked to see down the sights of their rifles. On the other side of the Antrim Road was where he believed the really bizarre and scary things went on. Ricky knew that several committed Republicans lived in his street but he was also aware of several residents who were Protestants, although these folk were mostly elderly. His mother told him that during the Ulster Workers Council Strike in 1974, as Loyalist protesters brought society to a standstill, Bob Henry, the Duncairn caretaker, had brought milk and bread into the street to distribute among his Catholic neighbours.

The trust was not the only benign influence on Ricky's life. He went to Holland with a scheme called 'Euro-children' which brought teenagers from inner-city environments to more peaceful locations in various parts of Europe in order to work and live together. For two months each year, Ricky lived on a farm near the Dutch city of Limburg. He had to mix with German and French teenagers and learn some basic communication in those two languages as well as trying to speak a few words in Dutch.

It was a relief to Ricky to head away for a while from the New Lodge, where a black taxi traveling in an unfamiliar direction along the usual Antrim Road taxi-route was enough to send him bolting along the street and into an entry for shelter, lest he be shot by a Loyalist. He could tell those locals who asked him why he hadn't joined the IRA's youth organization that he was 'moving any day to live in Holland'. There was pressure on him to become 'involved' with the IRA , as a 15 year old boy with a gift for electronics. He could have gone downtown any day and purchased components from which he could have made the timer for a bomb without the slightest difficulty.[36]

To live a better life

Another volunteer at the trust was Alan McBride. Like Tony Macaulay, he came from a nearby Loyalist area, in this case the Westland estate. Alan worked as a butcher in North Belfast and he made a Christian commitment at the age of 19, joining Antrim Road Baptist church where he met his future wife Sharon Frizell. On Alan's first night at the trust, Billy Kane tried to 'spook him out' by telling him that he was 'Dominic McGlinchey's brother'. 'Big Jim' McDonald, on hearing what was happening, told Billy to 'f----- off' and offered Alan protection. Alan stuck to Jim like glue for the rest of the night.

Looking back, Alan thinks that his motivation was simply to reach young Nationalists with 'the Christian message of personal salvation'. But eventually Alan found his mission framework challenged. He was troubled by the fact that some young people with whom he 'shared the gospel' were won over by its message and actually made professions of personal faith, then - as will be recounted in this narrative – they struggled to maintain this profession. How could they become part of a supportive Evangelical community without crossing the 'sectarian divide' and 'turning themselves into Protestants'? This step would make them outcasts from their own family and 'tribe'.

When volunteering in the New Lodge, Alan was also challenged by witnessing at first hand the antagonism between local people and the security forces, whereas the police and army were often regarded with respect in the community where Alan grew up.

He conversed at the Saltshaker with one young Republican who lived just a few yards away from the trust and was a frequent user of the cafe. Alan was challenged by this lad's criticisms of the Northern Ireland state, heard the case for a united, independent Ireland and listened as he spelt out the ethics and logic of an 'armed struggle'.[37]

This young Republican was not without knowledge of Ulster Protestant culture. His mother was Presbyterian and he had actually attended the Boys' Brigade in the Duncairn church.[38]

At 7pm on most evenings, volunteers would meet to pray for the local youths who would enter the Saltshaker that night. Then at 7.30, activities would begin. Often it was a matter of playing darts, pool or board games. Sometimes there was opportunity for deeper conversation. Occasionally, inspirational Christian speakers were brought along to give an address. One such person was Joe Campbell from the YMCA, who was good at re-telling the Easter story using a large wooden cross. During his talk, people were invited to write their names on a piece of paper and have that document nailed to the cross, after which the papers were burned. This vivid ritual, to illustrate Christ's death for each individual, made an impact on Alan.

(Alan tried to emulate Joe's talk at another venue, flamboyantly burning the pieces of paper to illustrate how the legacy of sin is destroyed by the power of Christ. Unfortunately, the flames got out of control and he ended up wielding a fiery cross that made him look like the Klu Klux Klan!)[39]

The regulars at the Saltshaker were mostly male, although quite a few girls did attend. Some of these male regulars, when looking back through the years, believe that New Lodge girls usually found the cafe and the back room too 'macho' an environment for their taste. Certainly the banter was fierce and a 'laddish' anarchy was never far from the surface. Often, when the Saltshaker was preparing to shut, the boys shouted 'Amity Shanks', which was the name of a famous toilet manufacturer, and then rushed into the 'loo'. They locked themselves in and refused to leave, singing a robust version of the civil rights anthem:

'We shall, we shall not be moved.

We shall, we shall not be moved.'[40]

The experience of the girls who came to the trust during these violent years is one of the untold sub-plots on the margins of this 174 narrative.

'Joe' was another lad who grew up in the New Lodge at this time.

Life for him was tough, frightening and thrilling. He found it hard to be a pupil at the local Catholic secondary school – St Patrick's – where bullying was a part of the schoolboy experience. However, St Patricks was still the place to go. All 'Joe''s friends were heading there so he deliberately tried to fail his 11+ examination, hoping he would not get sent to a grammar school.

'Joe' was hit twice by plastic bullets during his youth, despite being uninvolved in riots. But the ever-present danger was exciting. When living in one of the New Lodge tower-blocks, Joe and his friends would hear an explosion and look down to see where the bomb had gone off. If it was at a nearby shop, they scampered down to the bomb-site. Once the security forces had gone they would 'hoke around' in the rubble to find sweets or toys.

In the early years of the Troubles, when he was running around the streets, he developed a friendship with a boy from the Shankill. He used to 'sneak over' to see him. Then one day he went across, only to discover a barrier erected by the army, consisting of two massive fences with a short stretch of land in between, which would come to be known as the 'peace line'. On the far side of that wire stood his Protestant friend. And 'Joe' assumed, in a childlike way, that the fence had been put there to stop him and his friend from meeting.

Looking back he recognises that this sounds like a scene from a sentimental movie but he vouches for its absolute truth.

As he grew up and began to think for himself, these deep divisions seemed increasingly tragic and he never felt a desire to try to remedy the situation by fighting for a political cause. He had no love for Catholicism and he soon left church attendance behind. At the age of 17 he married a Protestant girl from the Shankill. They had met in the town centre. They settled in the New Lodge and raised a family. The conflict soon turned out to be less exciting than when he was a little boy. He lived with his young family on a volatile 'interface' with bullet-proof glass in the windows and a drop-bar on the door.[40]

Another lad connected to the New Lodge since 1969 was 'Sean'. In that year his family moved from East Belfast, where threats to members of his family had become unbearable. They lived in a flat in 'The Barrack' and 'Sean' attended St Malachy's Catholic Grammar School on the Lower Antrim Road before gaining admittance to Queens' University to read English and Philosophy. At that stage he was living in a flat in the university area during weekdays.

At one point, 'Sean' had been told that he was 'the right kind of young fella' to join the Fianna, but he did not want to get involved. However this scrupulous non-involvement did not stop him being stopped on a regular basis by some of the troops who patrolled the New Lodge. He has bad memories of one particular regiment who seemed keen on picking fights with the young men they stopped on the street. On countless occasions he had to answer probing questions about his identity, while a soldier ostentatiously loaded and aimed a rifle at him from nearby. 'Sean' recalls being taunted because he went to a grammar school, with the implication that he thought he was better than other people, including the soldiers. On another occasion he spent several hours undergoing a frightening interrogation in a nearby barracks.

For 'Sean' it is disturbing that both his grandfathers fought in the British Army in the Great War, serving for four years with the Connaught Rangers. One of his great-grandfathers also fought in this war and died in it. 'Sean' felt he was being unjustly treated as a 'terrorist' by members of that same army, just because of where he lived. However, he put these experiences behind him and trained as an English teacher, eventually working for several decades in a school elsewhere in Northern Ireland. Among his duties have been the pastoral care of his pupils and involvement in projects to build relationships between students from both sides of Northern Ireland's religiously divided school system.[42]

Johnny Owens was another young man who grew up in the New Lodge, his family residing four doors away from Billy Kane in Upper Meadow Street. He also attended St Malachy's Grammar School, which made him feel somewhat different from other lads in the Saltshaker. Before long he was focused on getting to university.

However his parents 'split up' when Jonny was 16 and he reacted by leaving home. His friend 'Tanto' told Jonny that Patton Taylor was prepared to offer him a place to 'kip' and so he knocked on the door of the Duncairn Manse. Jonny slept on the sofa in Patton's premises before he decided to return home. He still remembers this hospitality with favour.

Jonny Owens went regularly to the Saltshaker, took part in discussions in the cafe and the back room, attended the prayer meetings and volunteered to help with youth activities, gaining a certificate in youth work. He was a keen Catholic who attended Mass regularly throughout his teenage years, to the distaste of other boys who argued that the Catholic Church had become an enemy of Republicanism and that the Irish Catholic leaders were 'Brits' because they condemned the 'armed struggle'.

Like several young men at the cafe, Jonny decided to 'commit himself to Christ', hoping to experience a 'personal faith.' Jonny recognises that, back then, he wanted to be a 'better person' as did other New Lodge lads who were caught up in the chaotic circumstances of North Belfast.[43]

And undeniably, the Saltshaker leaders did seem to live a 'better life'. They served others voluntarily. Dave Maley would have given anyone his last penny. Tony and Lesley Macaulay's door was always open. Here were people who did not need to get drunk, who did not feel compelled to smoke and who thought of sex in exalted terms as something to be kept for marriage. They believed that reconciliation rather than confrontation was the way to solve Northern Ireland's problems. They were gentle role models.[44]

Jonny marvelled at how young the soldiers looked. Some seemed younger than him. He recalls one soldier who could have passed for 14 or 15. Jonny believes that many of them joined the ranks to get a job that would lift them off the streets of a Scottish or English city at a time when unemployment was sky-high.

Jonny's father and his Uncle Gerard had been in the British Army in the 1960s. For Mr Owens, the motivation was to find work, given that he had a family of six to feed. This experience in the army was a factor that made Jonny's dad oppose the 'armed struggle.' When Jonny's brother joined the IRA, his father disowned him. And when an IRA man came to 'borrow' the family car for an 'operation', Mr Owens refused and told them he voted for the Social Democratic and Labour Party, the Nationalist party that abjured force. Subsequently he found his car lying as a burnt-out wreck in the street.

Although Jonny never contemplated joining the IRA, he assisted his mates in building barricades. During the hunger-strikes, local boys built one barrier that had tragic consequences. A joy-rider in a stolen car swerved to avoid the obstacle and killed a local woman.

And Jonny knew all about teenage alcohol culture. All too often he stood in 'Phoenix Entry' opposite the trust, drinking Merrydown cider. He had been drinking and smoking since he was 13. But at the same time he focused on his school-work at St Malachy's, studied for '0-levels' then took History and Economics at 'A-level', before going to Queens University to study Psychology. He was always reluctant to take part in riots and end up in custody, gaining a 'criminal record'. But many of his friends followed this confrontational path, picked up by 'snatch squads' in the middle of a riot, then quite possibly sent to Palace Barracks in

Holywood for an interrogation.[45]

One other lad from the New Lodge who made the Saltshaker his home was Henry Davis from Atlantic Avenue. Billy Kane and Henry had been the first locals through the door in 1983 and they had been given free milkshakes as a result. Like most boys in the area, he had scarcely left Belfast and did not know what a holiday was. But he was familiar with all aspects of the war fought on his doorstep and knew the sounds of the weapons used by the combatants – the AK47, the M16, the SLR, the SA 80 and the RPG.

Initially Henry's contribution to the 'armed struggle' was to throw paint at the watchtower on a regular basis and avoid buckets of urine thrown out by the soldiers. Eventually he and his fiends became inventive, placing a suitcase full of soiled nappies and excrement on the pavement, then watching with glee as the army carried out a controlled explosion on this suspect device and the contents flew everywhere. On another occasion, the boys hoisted a sign onto the watchtower which said in bold letters – 'AIDS QUARANTINE CENTRE.'

The army sought their revenge. Henry recalls that on one occasion he and Billy were pulled into an entry by an army patrol. He recounts how the soldiers produced weapons that looked like Uzzi machine-guns, then mused aloud about whether to shoot the boys in the stomach, head or knees. Henry and Billy quaked with fear. The troops then revealed, amidst much mirth, that the 'Uzzis' were water-pistols. Then they let the two shaken captives go.

Ironically for Henry, as for Jonny and 'Sean', the British Army and his family history were inter-linked. Although his father was an ardent Republican and one of his relatives had fought in the War of Independence during the 1920s, another relative of Henry's was currently a bomb-disposal officer in the British Army and yet another relative had been a paratrooper in the Second World War, landing at Arnhem, where he had survived by hiding in a shell-hole under a pile of dead colleagues.[46]

Another young man who regularly used the Saltshaker was Pat Grogan. Pat had had little time for school, turning up each day at St Patrick's with his school-tie around his neck but little other concession to uniform. He carried the same jotter and pen to all the classes and did little work at any time. He and his brothers had lost their mother at an early age and, not long afterwards, their father had died too. The boys were 'farmed out' to relatives with whom Pat did not get on. In many ways, his sister's house was the closest thing to home but the Saltshaker was also a place of refuge.

By the time he was in his late teens, Pat was involved in riots and hijackings. On one occasion, he and a friend took over a lorry which was carrying a load of fruit. They decided they would distribute the cargo around the old people of the neighbourhood. This was a not uncommon practice. On another occasion, New Lodge youths commandeered a bread lorry and handed the contents out to the local people.

In due course, the trust tried to intervene radically in Pat's life, offering him a place to stay on the premises and a job, helping with the youth work, which might offer him some daily responsibility for others and give him a daily framework.[47]

Staring at the enemy

Someone who brought expertise and insight to youth work in this volatile environment was Maurice Kinkead. After training at the Irish Baptist College, he worked for the Frontier Youth Trust (FYT), which specialised throughout the UK in dealing with young people who lived in tough urban environments. FYT would be an important influence on youth work at 174 for many years.

Maurice had operated with young people in 'difficult' parts of Belfast but mainly in Protestant areas. In 1986 he was invited by Patton Taylor to join a committee which supervised the running of 174. He offered training to all the new volunteers and he also decided to 'volunteer' himself. In this way he would experience work 'on the ground' in the Saltshaker youth club.

As with many other key figures in the 174 story, Maurice's early life predisposed him towards openness to Nationalists. His early days had been spent in a uniformly Protestant part of Lurgan in County Armagh but during his teenage years the Kinkead family moved to Newcastle in County Down where Maurice encountered Catholic neighbours and made Catholic friends.

Maurice has vivid memories of discussions with young Nationalists on the 174 premises. He had to be well-informed about history and current affairs if he was going to engage. He recalls long meetings in Mary Malanaphy's flat, as the 174 committee tried to hammer out an agreed strategy. How could the trust express its faith in a community which was often imbued with a revolutionary political philosophy? This New Lodge radicalism challenged the status quo in Northern Ireland, a state whose current social and political construction most Ulster Evangelicals took for granted.

Many 174 leaders were also coming to see the reason for the discomfiting verdict pronounced by a volunteer in Patton Taylor's presence, back in the early 1980s:

'The real barriers between you and the kids is that you're all so middle-class and affluent.'

Maurice rarely felt thwarted by sectarian animosity during his work whereas he did feel that a huge barrier of class and behavioural culture had to be crossed, just as it did when operating in many Loyalist communities. The young people who appeared in the Saltshaker would have been classed as 'real bad boys' in many 'respectable' Ulster church circles. They would have been thrown out of most denominational youth clubs because they smoked and drank, cursed regularly as a part of everyday speech and had no respect for such pillars of society as the police or the education system. Learning to handle such youngsters with due respect was crucial.[48]

Another Frontier Youth Trust connection with the trust came through Kenny Groves. Kenny had been brought up in the Loyalist estate of Ballybeen. On coming to faith, he began to take an interest in youth work and participated in the 'Hob' initiative which reached out to young people in Holywood, County Down. He studied for a degree in Community Work at the University of Ulster and became the director of FYT in Northern Ireland. Kenny's future wife, Sarah Foster was a volunteer at the trust and she persuaded Kenny to get involved. In due course, he was asked by Patton to join the 174 board.[49]

Of course the young people of the New Lodge were not the only section of the community to benefit from the Christian volunteering which occurred at the trust. Hot dinners were carried to elderly people and to those who were housebound, using the 174 van. There were volunteers at work in the cafe kitchen on Christmas Day, preparing seasonal dinners for individuals who otherwise would spend the day alone.[50] Henry Davis moved from being a client of the trust to being a volunteer and then a paid worker. There was nothing he loved more than these Christmas morning experiences, when he felt he made a difference to peoples' lives and showed the true spirit of the season.[51] Often the meals had to be carried up the multiple stairways of the New Lodge tower-blocks.

Dinners for local pensioners were held during December in the Duncairn church hall. In the run-up to one particular Christmas, the turkey was burnt to a cinder in the 174 oven by a careless cook. A last-minute visit to the supermarket resulted in some rather inferior 'turkey roll' being purchased, which did not meet with the approval of the 'guests'.

On another Christmas, the pensioners asked if they could bring along some alcohol to drink with the meal but they were informed that 174 policy forbade the consumption of such beverages on the premises.

However as this meal progressed, the mood got more raucous. It became apparent that a few bottles of 'booze' had been stowed away in old ladies' handbags and that the contents were clandestinely poured into the Christmas orange juice.[52]

The danger which volunteers faced while working on the Antrim Road, is still imprinted on Maurice Kinkead's mind. To walk home to the Protestant streets of East Belfast from the 174 Trust after a late-night shift of work, was to risk assassination. This was a town where gunmen from Loyalist areas often stalked lone figures emerging from Nationalist areas. Yet Maurice was a member of a Protestant church who was working for the welfare of a Nationalist area. In doing so, he had come to accept other risks such as getting his car stolen. The car could have been taken by 'joy-riders' who were keen for illegal, dangerous fun or it might have been procured by IRA men, filled with high explosives and turned into a car-bomb, which would be left outside a targeted shop, government office or police station, somewhere across Northern Ireland.[53]

The 174 project-leaders made several attempts to bring teenagers together from 'both sides' of the Greater Belfast community. Tony and Lesley Macaulay decided to use their home as a venue where lads from the Saltshaker and boys from Lesley's Highfield youth project could meet and mix. On the first occasion, the two groups sat on either side of the room as if staring at the enemy across No Man's Land. Gradually they mingled. They were motivated, as Lesley recalls, by sheer curiosity about one another.

Later, at a 'neutral' community venue on the upper Antrim Road, discussions started. Sometimes angry words were exchanged and accusations made. However when anyone spoke of a family member or friend who had died or been injured in the 'Troubles', respect was shown. In fact, every single member of the two groups had lost someone in the conflict. Very often, stories of loss and grief were delivered with a remarkable lack of bitterness.

But the two youth groups joined up for more cheerful activities such as football outings to Ballysillan Leisure Centre, a short distance away from 174. Other experiments with 'cross community' youth work took place, including joint meetings with Protestant teenagers from the Hob in Hollywood.[54]

If God cries for Belfast

Long-term volunteers from the USA began to feature. One such volunteer was Dave Moser, who arrived in Belfast in 1987, as the first worker that the Mennonite Church had ever sent to Northern Ireland. The Mennonite tradition has its origins in the radical reformation practices of the Anabaptists and is rooted in rejection of violence and a belief in discursive conflict resolution, so a volunteer such as Dave possessed values which were going to be relevant to a conflicted society such as Northern Ireland. He was given a three year assignment at 174.

In August, he left Indiana with the words of an old Mennonite saying ringing in his ears:

'The word and the deed are one.'

He arrived into Belfast International Airport, marveling at the green fields he had seen from the descending aircraft. He can still remember Tony Macaulay picking him up at the airport in a blue Ford van that the trust owned at the time.

Dave was taken to his new home on the Cliftonville Road, not far from the trust. He moved in with other workers such as Bill Fleming, Keith Spears, and John Frizell. Coming from small-town 'Midwest America', this sojourn in North Belfast involved cultural adjustment. Bill Fleming has since confided to Dave that he thought he wouldn't last more than a month before flying back to 'the States'.

As Dave has recently recalled:

'When I first came to Belfast in 1987, there were very few American volunteers that I knew of in Northern Ireland…..I recall Alan McBride asking me when he first met me –

'What is a Mennonite? Is that some kind of Old Testament tribe like the Hittites or the Amorites, or something?'

Dave also struggled with the Northern Irish pronunciation during those first few weeks and admitted in his diary to understanding only one in four words.[55] But he would have had no trouble making out what one of the 'lads' said when this new American first walked into the café :

'F-----, you're big!'[56]

It was an understandable reaction, given that Dave was almost 6 feet and 7 inches in height.

Dave found it hard to grasp the religious language used in Northern Ireland, especially the local term for conversion to faith - 'getting saved.' Before long he was making friends with Alan, with Dave Maley, with Heather Reid, Karen Pauley and Kate Hunter. And he was soon invited into the lives of the 'lads', as the youths who visited the centre were fondly called. Henry Davis also stayed at the house in the Cliftonville Road, while working at the trust. Dave got to know him well.

And he was soon aware of the affiliations of the locals. He made his first trip to a local pub with the 'lads', and although he did not touch any alcohol, he saw one of his drinking–partners take a pint of Guinness and write 'IRA' in the white foam, to show the American guest. And Dave soon became aware of the dangers that loomed. Henry Davis turned up at the house one night and warned Dave to keep the door shut as a Catholic had just been killed at the bottom of the road and the atmosphere was very tense.

On Dave's first day at the after-school Bible club for younger kids, there were children standing outside the front of the building, waiting for him to unlock the door and let them in. Then an army foot patrol went past. An IRA gunman, hiding in a house across the street, fired several shots at the British troops. Dave immediately rushed the children inside and made them lie on the floor under the tables. The shooting did not last long but as soon as the firing stopped, several young men started throwing rocks and bottles at the soldiers, from across the street.

This introduction to the street-life of the New Lodge was a massive shock:

'Prior to coming to Belfast, I had just finished doing my teacher training in a school in Indiana called Honeyville - a tiny place out in the middle of farming country. The school was small. Every last one of the students at Honeyville were Amish children. They all lived on farms, they came from families that drove horse and buggies, and were a part of a church and a way of life that espouses simplicity of life, peace, and humility. I came from doing my student teaching in this idyllic setting where violence was something that "happened somewhere else." I had now landed in "the somewhere else" where violence was a daily occurrence.'

Writing home to his folks in Indiana, Dave looked at the hills above the city and thought:

'I wonder if God ever stands on top of Cave Hill and cries for the city of Belfast.'

Before long he was conscious of 174's unusual and potentially controversial status. He was aware that it could well be perceived as a Protestant organization operating outside its territorial remit within a Catholic area. He wondered how the Catholic clergy perceived the trust and heard rumours that Irish priests were well used to the phenomenon of Evangelical influence on their flock. The priests were familiar with the phrase 'born again' which was used to denote an Evangelical conversion.

Dave was told that the priests wryly categorized 'born again' Catholics as BA1s. BA2s and BA3s. The first were 'born again' but still going exclusively to the Catholic chapel. The second were 'born again' but belonging to an ecumenical fellowship group as well as going to Mass. The third had 'moved across', after being 'born again', in order to join a Protestant denomination. However, although the Catholic clergy seemed to keep well away from the trust, where the concept of being 'born again' had currency, they did not seem to disapprove of its existence.

Dave was the 'Youth Work Coordinator' at 174. He did not doubt the danger that the trust's workers faced at times of tension. Despite the IRA's prohibition of violence against the trust, petrol bombs had been thrown at the building on one occasion but had failed to explode. The management did not want to pursue the matter further, either with the police or with Sinn Fein, the political party that allied itself with the IRA. To liaise with the Royal Ulster Constabulary would be seen as treachery. To take the matter to the local leaders of Sinn Fein would be to risk the possibility that the IRA would then deal with the culprits. This might involve a severe physical punishment, which would compromise the trust's peaceful witness.

Dave got used to the New Lodge on that first winter in Northern Ireland. Occasionally he took Patton's Irish setter for a walk through the streets in the cold morning air. And he wrote home, describing some of the eerie night-time scenes. On one occasion, as he started to walk home towards 218 Cliftonville Road, he witnessed the aftermath of a riot –

'a light flashed blue across the pavement, and at the front corner of the church, a group of soldiers were on guard, pointing their high-powered guns at a few of the lads drinking in front of a closed bar. At the top of the New Lodge Road, there were faint flames still burning in a charred van. It was a surreal scene.'[57]

It wasn't long before events in Northern Ireland caught the eyes of the rest of the world. In November 1987, the IRA exploded a bomb at a Remembrance Day service in Enniskillen, seeing it as a ritual of veneration for the British Army. Civilians who had come to take part in the event were killed and injured. All across the world, and indeed within Republican circles, there was a strong sense that the universally sacred process of paying homage to the dead had been violated by the bombing. The consequences were felt within hours on the Antrim Road, when Loyalists combatants opened fire at a group of young men who were standing in the street. Several teenage boys were injured.[58]

In the weeks to come, Dave got to know one of the boys who had been shot. He could be seen making his way along the road with the help of crutches.

Despite these grim events, Dave felt encouraged by some things. He had got to know some local lads who, because of their conversations in the Saltshaker's back room, had decided to try the pathway of personal faith. One of them said to Dave:

'I used to be happy about things like Enniskillen, but I now have a spirit that makes me feel sad for them'.

Another lad told him, after the shooting of the local teenagers:

'We must forgive the gunmen and pray for them.'

So Dave concluded in one of his weekly letters home –

'I have seen people turn to love from violence....there is hope in a God who acts through individuals and changes people where they are...' [59]

Take my hatred away

Dave Moser would certainly have been encouraged by the story of Josey Grogan. Josey had been behind bars from 1983 to 1987. On his release he met Billy Kane, who told him about the Saltshaker. Before long, Josey was a 174 regular. He enjoyed meeting people he could never have encountered before, such as the volunteer Bill Fleming, with his shaven head, his rural County Down accent and his openness about the extreme right-wing views he had held not so long ago.

Josey had never been religious and he tended to view the churches, with all their apparent opulence, as the robbers of the poor. Now he had come across a different kind of religion. The 174 volunteers seemed selfless and they appeared happy. Soon he aspired to be like them. He volunteered to work at the trust and he made a point of attending the worship meetings which were held each day in the room behind the café.

Eventually he was given a chance to run his own projects and was paid through the ACE scheme for his work. He got a local man to come and deliver an electronics class, he set up a bingo night for the 'older ladies' and he led summer projects for the children, whom he took to a nearby swimming pool or to Lady Dickson Park for outdoor games. There was even a 174 Trust football team, complete with female cheerleaders.[60]

Other volunteers from the United States arrived to help run the summer schemes. They included Chris Rogers who had joined a project offered by his church in Seattle, which enabled young people to travel in their summer vacation and engage in Christian mission within challenging locations. Chris headed for a summer project based in the 174 Trust and at Lucan in the Irish Republic. Ireland was a welcome location because his grandmother had come from the town of Ballymena. He also hoped that 'learning from a different culture' while 'serving other people' would 'shape and grow' his faith.

Chris was struck by many things about Belfast, including the Victorian architecture, the Army's grim-looking fortresses and the vivid political graffiti on the walls. He was impressed by the long-term volunteers and staff at the trust. He felt they were 'committed to playing a part in healing their nation'. He loved to listen to their stories about life in the New Lodge and he was struck by the strange, courageous relish with which the children of the area:

'shared their brush with the Troubles – a family member who had died or been injured, or their own scares with sectarian gang warfare.'

He was especially struck by the way in which, despite the sombre realities of inner-city Belfast, spontaneous and joyful musical sessions took place at the end of 174 outings to local parks or football games. Chris saw 'great musical talent pop up everywhere' with 'guitars, tin whistles, great voices and dance' all in evidence. Some of the most exultant sessions took place in the evening, when a 'fun day out' concluded with a picnic. Everyone joined in, including children, teenagers, leaders and volunteers from abroad. The repertoire included Christian praise songs, Irish ballads and pieces freshly written by local musicians.

One talented young man that Chris knew as 'Jim' performed his own songs about life in the New Lodge and about his own struggle to forgive the wrongs he had seen done to his community. One song which spelt out his feelings contained a plea to God to 'take my hatred away.'

On one frightening occasion, while walking down the 'Murder Mile' in darkness, Chris found himself being picked out in the beam of a laser scope. This was a device which enabled British fire to be targeted onto the body of a suspected gunman by means of a pinpoint of light. As Chris watched, a laser pinpoint moved across his chest. It was directed from a foot patrol crouching in the shadows on the other side of the street. He finally reached home, safe but deeply terrified.

Years later, when interviewed by the author of this narrative and working as a financial advisor in his home town of Seattle, Chris Rogers still considered his short time in Ireland as very formative. He spent four years on his church's staff, after leaving college, inspired in part by the 174 experience of 'comprehensive community service'.

In due course, Chris left his Christian faith behind, feeling that a world-view based on the idea of a loving creator no longer made sense. By 2009 he described himself as a 'reluctant agnostic' who only holds to the possibility of a God. He expressed his belief in caring for others and devoting some time and income to community projects, both in his own city and overseas.

Chris asserted that he still admired the selfless love shown by many Christians and said that he was grateful for the way in which his years of faith shaped his character and the rest of his life.[61]

Hope and wholeness

Mary Malanaphy, the first director of the trust, had moved to Dublin in 1985 to live with her new husband.[62] The trust then came under the supervision of the Welshman and former Baptist pastor, John Evans. He continued the work for which 174 had become known in the area and he gained much respect.[63] One major feature of the outreach was the 174 Trust Disability Project. This was relevant in a part of the city where facilities were meagre and the incidence of disability high.

Two key figures in that work were husband and wife, Jim and Deena Nimick, who had made their first contact with the 174 Trust in the early 1980s as volunteers in the summer schemes and youth clubs. They later returned to undertake paid work within 174, developing a 'befriending scheme' and expanding the local 'PHAB' Club (Physically Handicapped but Able Bodied) This was a club that had been established by Philip McClean. It provided a much needed social outlet for adults who had severe disabilities and illnesses.

Jim and Deena continued to 'job-share' for the following 12 years and throughout this time, with the support from a large group of committed volunteers, the work expanded. An Adult Carers' Social Group was established. The local offices of the government-run Social Services then approached them to ask if they would set up a junior PHAB Club. This junior club provided disabled and chronically ill youngsters with the opportunity to enjoy activities alongside their non-disabled peers in a safe and secure environment.

Later the Social Services asked the leaders of the project to set up a Young Carers' Support Group for children of primary school age. This 'NOMO' (Not On My Own) activity group was aimed at young children who were handling difficult domestic circumstances because a parent or sibling had a disability, illness or addiction. Soon after this, additional finance was also sourced to provide support and developmental opportunities for teenage carers. So an organization called 'YCAP' was created, dedicated to their needs.

When interviewed in 2008, Deena explained how many local people had had little trust in the government-run Social Services. Thus it was often said that the 174 projects were a lifeline for disabled people and carers in inner-city North Belfast, as genuine trust was built with 174 staff and volunteers. This good relationship was due to the great emphasis placed at 174 on the nurture and empowerment of local disabled people and also their carers. Close networks and friendships were established through which practical care could be given, a listening ear provided and a sense of solidarity maintained.

174 enriched Deena's faith. Years later, she could still recall early-morning prayer times at the Saltshaker when the needs of the New Lodge were 'brought before the Lord'. Out and about in the community, she found many people who were grateful to God for His blessings, even in the direst circumstances. She was inspired by how men and women coped with extreme suffering and 'gained inner strength from the Lord'. She saw how many people retained hope in this life along with a strong belief in a better future in the life to come.

Coming from a Protestant part of East Belfast, Deena loved the new relationships she developed in the New Lodge. When spiritual issues did emerge in conversation, she found that most Catholic (or post-Catholic) people manifested a more 'open heart' than many people from her own part of the city, who appeared to have become indifferent to the Christian message that had been 'drummed into them' from an early age.

She felt safe and 'looked after' on the lower Antrim Road. In the early days when buses were burning in the New Lodge and riots were raging, locals would go out of their way to tell her which homeward route to take in order to avoid getting caught up in the violence.

During their time at the 174 Trust, Jim and Deena enjoyed the birth of their three children. However they were devastated when their second child, Sophia, was diagnosed as having leukaemia. Sophia died after a four-year traumatic battle with the illness. On their return to 174 after Sophia's death, Jim and Deena were determined to share the 'great hope and strength that God had given them' through the ups and downs of Sophia's illness and her eventual passing. A set of 'Hope and Wholeness' services was set up, where intercessors from both Protestant and Catholic backgrounds met with individuals to offer prayer for whatever was causing them concern or pain.

In 2008, Deena looked back with regret on those times at the 174 Trust when conflict broke out over the direction that the organization ought to choose, when management was suddenly changed, when funding dried up and when jobs were lost. She has also expressed her sadness that 174 had lost its strong evangelistic ethos. But, when thinking about the many years spent at the trust, she said that she was, nonetheless:

‘greatly encouraged by how the Lord continued to bless and expand His work within the community.’ [64]

Hey, mad-dog!

Bill Fleming, who shared a house with Dave Moser, was a well-known figure at the trust. He had arrived at the New Lodge to work on a summer scheme in 1986 on the advice of his girlfriend Lorraine who had already experienced the project. Bill was from a Loyalist background in Banbridge. He had attended the local grammar school where he had developed such extreme right-wing political views that one of his teachers dubbed him ‘Gauleiter Fleming’. An Evangelical conversion led him to seek membership of Banbridge Baptist Church and stimulated him in ways that would eventually lead to a change of politics.

Before long Bill was searching for a spiritual challenge. He was a ‘bookworm’ and curious to read everything he could get his hands on. As Bill himself expresses it, he would have ‘read the label on a sauce-bottle’. He was fascinated by the writings of radical Christian thinkers such as Tony Campolo. After taking on the challenge of that first summer scheme he decided to become a 174 volunteer, residing at premises on the Cliftonville Road and helping with youth work in the evenings, while operating as a trainee accountant during the day.

When he was walking home along the Cliftonville Road, which was a highway known in local parlance as the ‘Murder Mile’, Bill knew a level of fear he had not experienced in the relatively quiet County Down town of Banbridge. He always had his route marked out with various ‘bolt-holes’ - alleyways, entries and driveways en route, where he could bolt for safety if the driver of a car slowed down behind him with murderous intent.

Several local jokers used to slow down behind pedestrians, just to give them a fright. The occupants of the vehicle could be heard laughing, as it drove off again. Sometimes Bill could hardly get the key into the keyhole of the front door as his hand was shaking so badly. The inmates of 218 Cliftonville Road were reluctant to go down to the corner shop for milk after dark. But sometimes Bill decided to take a chance. On the way back he would clutch the bottle in his hand, ready to use his ‘pinta’ as a feeble improvised missile, if anyone pointed a gun at him.

And meeting the Saltshaker regulars was a new kind of experience. One lad walked into the café on Bill’s first day, wearing a T-shirt which proclaimed that Superman was in the IRA.

But the only physical force tradition that interested Bill was boxing. A love of the sport was 'in his family' and immediately he arrived at 174 he asked where the local boxing clubs were. Billy Kane, who was ever one to oblige, took Bill to a club to see the 'action'. On the walls of his room at 218 Cliftonville Road, Bill soon erected posters of his boxing heroes such as 'Hit-man' Hearns. When Dave Moser's Mennonite friends turned up in Belfast, he contemplated the effect of these images on their pacifist sensibilities and kept his door firmly shut before making the self-sacrificial decision to take the posters (temporarily) down.

Bill rejoiced in a New Lodge nick name. The lads thought it funny to call a Christian volunteer something inappropriate so they named him 'Mad Dog.' On one occasion, on a youth residential weekend at a sedate hotel in the seaside resort of Bangor, Jim Corry, who was distraught at the absence of his favourite breakfast cereal , yelled across a crowded dining-room:

'Hey , Mad Dog, there's no coco-pops!'

The hotel guests stared in horror at Bill, convinced that he was a brutal gangland god-father.

Bill became a Saltshaker favourite on his return from Banbridge every Sunday night. His mother worked in a bakery and she gave Bill the 'leftover' buns and cakes to take back to the city. They soon disappeared when the clients of the café got their hands on them.

But he became wary of some aspects of the 174 enterprise. He found educational materials which were being used by one or two other volunteers and which peddled a rather rigid Protestantism, seeking to inform young people of the 'fundamental errors of the Catholic church.' He also gathered that Dave Maley was causing a stir by attending a Catholic chapel rather than a Protestant church as had been tacitly 'agreed' as part of his 'contract.' To Bill's mingled amusement and consternation, he also found mail which had was injudiciously addressed to the ' 174 Catholic Outreach Centre.'

But despite these fears and frustrations, Bill reckons that he has never laughed so hard as he did during his '174 years'. The verbal quips of Patton's ministerial assistant David Templeton were a source of mirth. He was the person who felt most up to the job of 'taking the hand' out of his boss, making jokes about Patton's interest in the Territorial Army and accusing him of playing at tin-pot soldiers. Patton in turn, played a few practical jokes on his workers.

Like the other workers at the trust, Bill was impressed by the friendship shown by the 'lads,' despite their tough demeanour and shocking views. They were protective of Bill and his partner Lorraine. On one occasion they escorted her down to the unemployment office in Corporation Street, to claim the benefits to which she was entitled as a student. The official behind the desk could not comprehend what this 'nice' girl with a broad country accent was doing surrounded by a posse of 'wee Belfast hard men'.

However the rampant machismo of the New Lodge streets also intrigued Bill along with the vulnerability that underlay it. On one occasion, he led his lads on a somewhat surreal pilgrimage to a nearby Blood Transfusion Unit. On arriving back at the trust, one young man who had a 'hard' image, came into Bill's office and asked if he could lie down because he was feeling faint. What also terrified this lad was that he might collapse in front of the others, a demonstration of frailty that he would never live down.

Bill suspected that there was even a reluctant admiration for spectacular behaviour by the British Army. The same lad who had feared fainting after his blood donation told Bill that he had seen the massed ranks of one particular regiment advancing onto the Antrim Road from the surrounding side-streets, while beating their batons in unison on their riot-shields, like a scene from a film about the Zulu Wars.

'It was wonderful!' he said. 'My two knees were shaking against each other! [65]

How can a person live in this country?

In the late 1980s and the early 1990s a 'Peace Process' began to unfold behind the scenes, in which the British and Irish governments and many of the local players in the conflict began to talk to each other about a cessation of hostilities. They discussed an end to the Loyalist and Republican military campaigns, a massive reduction of the security force presence and new structures of government that would command the respect of most local citizens. The first major results of such dialogue were the Republican and Loyalist ceasefires of 1994. Subsequently, in 1998, the Good Friday Agreement resulted in the initiation of a power-sharing regime in Northern Ireland, in which most local politicians were willing to participate.[66]

However the reconciliatory developments of the mid-1990s were still a long way off on the streets of North Belfast as the year 1988 began.

In January, growing more ambitious, Dave Moser tried to organize a cross-community football game for 7 and 8 year-old boys from different parts of the city. It was a disaster as the youngsters turned up in football tops that immediately spelt out their allegiances. In the polarized world of 1980s Belfast, anyone wearing a Glasgow Celtic or Cliftonville football top was clearly a Catholic and anyone wearing a Glasgow Rangers shirt or the colours of Linfield FC was marked out as a Protestant. Even at an early age, as Dave now realized, deep antagonism affected many of Belfast's children. The football game had to be abandoned, due to the hostility of the little boys towards one another.

During the winter months, Dave and Tony Macaulay pursued plans to send some of the Saltshaker lads to Indiana for a break from the daily stresses of Belfast. Hopefully a spell in the USA would open their eyes to other possibilities than life on 'the dole' and a daily confrontation with the British Army. Dave and Tony were particularly keen to persuade Billy Kane to travel to the States as he seemed a fragile young man, underneath his tough-talking exterior and his regular confrontations with the army, which was so clearly motivated by his tragic family history. Dave wrote to Mennonite friends at home and described Billy –

'His future plans are grim.....is there a family that would be willing to risk a lot and give a lot for Billy? You would be surprised at his soft side.'[67]

However, when Dave tried to get Billy to leave this torture behind and move to Indiana for a while, he turned it down. He spoke of trying hard to find a job and he talked about his girlfriend and their plans to marry. In reality, Dave and Tony knew that the thought of moving away from the painful familiarities of the New Lodge to the unknown freedom of Indiana was just too much for him to contemplate.

On January 15th 1988, Billy walked from his home in Upper Meadow Street to the Saltshaker café in order to have something to eat and to enjoy a chat. On the menu was his favourite dish – baked beans on toast. His friends knew he was often prone to dark moods but on this particular afternoon he seemed in good form. His was joined by his brother Eddy and a few other lads. His friend Joe McGuigan saw Billy looking across the café to where Bill Fleming was tucking into a massive plate of 'grub'. Billy shouted out:

'Hey Bill, are you going to eat that food or jump over it?'[68]

Dave Moser also saw Billy in the café that afternoon. He watched him take little Sarah on his knee – the daughter of one of the café staff – and feed her with chips and a sip of Coke. Turning to Dave, as he cuddled the child, he called out:

'Look, she loves me...'[69]

Shortly afterwards, Billy paid a visit to a snooker hall where Pat Grogan was playing and then returned to Upper Meadow Street and fell asleep for a while on the sofa in his living room, in front of the television.[70] He had agreed with Henry Davis that the lads would head out to the pub later that night and go into the city centre and have some fun.[71]

Meanwhile, Jonny Owens was walking home along Upper Meadow Street from the chip shop with hot food for the tea. He heard shots ring out and in the darkness he vaguely saw two men rushing out of the Kane home and into a car which sped away. Terrified by what he had witnessed, Jonny went into his house for shelter but soon he heard screaming and the sound of neighbours gathering outside the Kanes' door, followed by the wailing sirens of police vehicles and an ambulance.

Jonny soon learnt that the men he had glimpsed fleeing from the scene of the shooting had walked into the house and fired several bullets into Billy's chest, in front of his mother and sisters. By the time the ambulance and police had arrived, Billy was dead and the gunmen had long since disappeared.[72]

The Kane family was convulsed by shock and grief. For Billy's mother, this was a nightmarish sequel to the events of 1971, when her husband had perished in the explosion at McGurk's bar on North Queen Street.[73]

That night, Joe McGuigan was watching the TV news in a friend's house in another part of the city and discovered that someone had been just been killed by Loyalist gunmen in the New Lodge. Soon he learnt that that 'someone' was his friend Billy. He could not believe how swiftly the whole ghastly episode had unfolded.[74]

The Saltshaker closed in silence. The tension in the air was palpable. Upper Meadow Street had justified, yet again, the grim nickname 'Upper Murder Street', awarded because of the number of fatalities associated with it.[75]

That night, Dave Moser recorded his distress within his diary. He looked out of his window and saw helicopters droning in the sky over the New Lodge, pointing their searchlights down at the narrow city streets. He wrote:

'....I won't be able to read Billy my letters anymore to cheer him up, Laura won't be able to complain about him leaving without paying for his meals, he won't be in the corner any more with his feet propped up on the table, looking cool in his green, red and blue coat and there won't be the same "Hey man!" yelled across the street...'[76]

Meanwhile Pat Grogan was desperately trying to contact Bill Fleming, in order to break the news. Bill had gone home to Banbridge for the weekend. Pat ended up leafing through the phone book and picking on what looked like a suitable number. He managed to get through to Bill's mother, who could only sympathise with Pat and tell him that her son was out, but he would be informed as soon as he got in.[77]

In due course, the Saltshaker volunteers came to the wake and shared in the Kane family's mourning. Josey Grogan recalls seeing Alan McBride standing crying in Billy's house.[78] A few days later, the funeral took place and workers and customers from the trust gathered in Upper Meadow Street to walk behind the coffin.[79] Dave recorded in his diary –

'There were 1,000 people walking along behind Billy and his close friends carried him part of the way. The Bishop said good things about peace and love - Billy would have walked out of the church had he been alive!'

Later that evening, Dave heard 'Tanzy' Campbell say:

'How can a person live in this country?'

Then another person told him:

'...this place will never change. It will be this way when I die and the same 100 years after I am gone.'

To try and express their grief, a couple of the Saltshaker regulars got together and composed a 'Song for Billy', which began:

'Sad eyes...you had those sad eyes...'

Meanwhile Dave Moser wrote in his diary that he had seen 'the wrong Billy, cold in a wooden box' when he had visited the wake, a couple of days before in Upper Meadow Street. The corpse bore no resemblance to the angry young lad he had come to know. Dave reflected darkly that, despite his Christian faith, he had had nothing of worth to say to the family:

'What can you say to a sister who in vain tries to breathe life back into her brother but the air just keeps coming out the holes in his chest?.... sometimes I wish I could go back to an easy armchair faith...I can never be the same again.'

Dave explained to his parents in Indiana how he could still recall all the little details connected with Billy, such as the way his black shoes marked the tops of the Saltshaker tables. Dave told them that despite having known Billy such a short time, he was grieving deeply for him –

'A part of you has died with your friend. It goes beyond more grey hair. I think my very soul is greyer.'

On January 27th, Dave wrote that a number of the lads who frequented the Saltshaker café had been 'lifted' for rioting and armed hijacking in the aftermath of Billy's death. Taken to court, clad in handcuffs, they were now out on bail but facing an extended gaol sentence.[80]

In truth, some of the 'lads' had been so suffused with rage in the hours after the killing that they had vowed to drive to a Loyalist area and 'take out' the entire clientele of a crowded bar. Henry Davis looks back with relief at the fact that he was soon arrested on charges to do with riotous behaviour, as it meant that he did not get to express his anger in a more deadly manner, with all the suffering it would have brought to the victims and the subsequent guilt with which he would have had to live.[81]

For the entire Saltshaker community, Billy's death was a bleak experience. Lesley Macauley was still working in the Loyalist Highfield estate and she was due to be a guest speaker at the daily 'assembly' in Cairnmartin Secondary School just a few days after the funeral. She resolved to use the opportunity to share her distress with the audience of several hundred boys from the Greater Shankill catchment area.

She decided to deliver a monologue that would tell the story of Billy's short life and his violent death. She proceeded to deliver it in a voice shaking with emotion. The assembled ranks in the hall became totally silent. Still fighting back the tears, she said a prayer for peace and healing. When she had finished, the boys filed out of the hall without a word being said.

A few minutes later, she received a call to the headmaster's office. Lesley was scared that she would receive a negative response to her very emotional contribution. However she was relieved to learn that the headmaster was deeply touched by her talk. He said it was the only time that he had ever witnessed his pupils passing out of the assembly hall in total silence.[82]

For many of the local lads in the Saltshaker, this was a difficult time. Some were waiting to hear a date for their court appearance and all were grieving in their own way for Billy.[83]

Riots still happened episodically through the early months of 1988. Dave Moser watched some boys leave the café, saying 'I've got work to do…' Moments later they were involved in confrontation with the security forces, throwing missiles and facing plastic bullets. He wrote home to his family, describing one youngster who had been hit in the face by a plastic bullet:

'It nearly took his nose off. His whole face was black and blue and swollen. All his teeth were crushed back in his face. On Friday he had all his teeth pulled out. He is 16 and wearing false teeth to death.'[84]

Added to all of this, the situation throughout the country was more tense than at any time since the hunger-strikes. The killing of three unarmed IRA volunteers in Gibraltar by a British 'special forces' unit was followed by an assault on the IRA funeral in West Belfast's Milltown cemetery by self-styled 'freelance' Loyalist activist Michael

Stone. Subsequently, as the funeral of those killed in Milltown passed through West Belfast, two soldiers in plain clothes were apprehended by a crowd of mourners and shot dead.[85]

The budding Christian spirituality of some young men in the New Lodge could not survive the pain of it all.

Dave was close to one Saltshaker regular who had shown deep interest in Evangelical Christianity during the previous year but had then gone back on the street as an angry protestor after Billy died. Now he seemed determined to put behind him the pain of his recent interrogation by the security forces. He wished to face the likelihood of gaol with calm fortitude.

After visiting his house to chat, Dave realised the pressure that his friend was facing and cried for him on the way home. A few weeks later, as the New Lodge lads awaited their court hearing and Northern Ireland lurched through the crisis that followed the Gibraltar killings, this young man again sought Dave out. He told him he had now decided to give up on faith, saying:

'It does not work in this country. Love does not work. In a matter of days everything has changed.'

Shortly after this, he and a few of his mates arrived at 218 Cliftonville Road, where Dave resided. They sang songs, drank beer and created an affray in front of the house, which led to an intervention by the police.

Dave Moser had found out just how hard it was to sustain a Christian commitment and to live by an ethic of love and peace, for young men who were existing in the midst of a bitter and confusing war on the lower Antrim Road. Incarceration was only going to make things tougher. Henry Davis, for instance, faced nine charges. He would consider himself very lucky when the judge gave him a mere two and a half years. This was a sentence which, through good behaviour, he managed to reduce to 18 months.

A generation of ACE Christians

Dave Moser had arrived in Belfast as a single person but a year after this his friend Beth Bowman came over to holiday with him in the city. Their relationship had been blossoming, despite being conducted by letter. They now made plans for marriage in America in 1989, after which they would return together to Northern Ireland.

Dave would continue to volunteer at the Saltshaker and Beth would be placed by Mennonite Missions in another venue. This turned out to be the YMCA in central Belfast, where she would work in health education, dealing with addiction and with the new phenomenon of AIDS.

Beth and Dave were married in May 1989. The young couple started life together in a rented house in Castleton Gardens, further along the Antrim Road. On Sundays, Dave and Beth attended a Quaker meeting-house. On weekdays, Dave rode his bike to the Saltshaker and Beth travelled into town to her office at the YMCA as she tried to come to terms with a new culture and a very different country.

By now, the 174 Trust faced internal problems. Money was scarce. At one stage the trust's van had to be got rid of as it was costing too much. The youth club funds were down to zero and the trust possessed a number of unpaid debts. Workers came and left with regularity. There were theological disagreements and there were personality clashes. One tragedy concerned a young man who did some work at the trust and who had been involved in substance abuse. Since making a profession of faith, he had tried to practise a healing ministry with North Belfast's drug addicts but then reverted to his old habits and died of an overdose.

Meanwhile, in the leadership of the trust there was change. John Evans left the scene very swiftly in October 1989. He had been a troubled man for some time but no-one expected the cryptic note which read:

'By the time you read this I'll be living in England.'

In an editorial in the next edition of the Saltshaker newspaper, Patton Taylor wrote:

'We pray that God will speak to John, wherever he is now and guide him during this period…'

Bill Fleming took on the temporary role of acting director until he was replaced in 1990 by Derek McCorkell, who moved into a house on the Cliftonville Road with his family.[86]

Meanwhile a decision was made by the 174 management to 'downsize' the organization. Many in the management team felt it was becoming a logistic and financial headache to run. The fact that a cheque of £200,000 arrived in the 174 Trust's lap in order to run the ACE scheme was a mixed blessing. Patton Taylor felt that it distracted the organization from the hard work required to raise the much smaller sum of £20,000 which was needed to sustain the Christian volunteers and help pay a few modestly salaried staff, to meet the Saltshaker bills and to get the summer outreach schemes underway. There was the moral and managerial anomaly of an organization in which voluntary labour, paid work and government-funded 'ACE' jobs took place side by side.[87]

Redundancies occurred at the Saltshaker, to the grief of those who now lost work in recession-hit times. For people who were now on the management committee - such as Tony Macaulay - the task of informing the paid staff of redundancies was a tough one.

The 'ACE' scheme, run by Philip McClean, had become, in the committee's eyes, too demanding a project to host at the cramped Saltshaker offices. And though it offered short-term gains to local people, many of whom kept on re-applying for 'ACE' funding, some members of the management board felt it was doing little to spread the Christian gospel of personal regeneration and enduring uplift in the New Lodge.

Tony Macaulay was aware of 'Rice Christians' who, in Asian missionary work, underwent conversion merely to reap the benefits of regular food. He wondered if the 174 Trust was creating a generation of 'ACE Christians' who were happy to be associated with the Saltshaker mainly in order to procure their regular episodes of employment.[88]

Philip McClean's large ACE unit was moved from the 174 premises and established in offices elsewhere in North Belfast although some ACE workers were still employed by the trust. In truth, Philip was glad of the move, as this narrative will later reveal.[89]

Meanwhile the summer schemes continued to be popular with local young people and the volunteers who staffed them. Many scary but amusing incidents took place. A visit to Belfast Zoo was part of the itinerary and on one occasion a pair of hyper-active New Lodge twins was lost from the party, only to be found inside an enclosure belonging to the prairie dogs.

Jokes later went around that the prairie dogs had had to be rescued.[90]

Louise McDowell was a volunteer in 1989 and 1990, while making the transition from being a 6th form pupil at a Belfast school, to working as a trainee nurse. Patton Taylor led Louise's team, which included new workers who had arrived from England and the USA, including some Mennonites following in Dave Moser's footsteps.

She recalls how the young volunteers slept in the church halls and she can remember bringing two Americans to her parents' house in a more comfortable part of North Belfast, to get their washing done and have an afternoon's sleep in a proper bed.

She recollects how the Duncairn church halls were used each morning for childrens' activities while the coffee bar was opened in the evening for the older youth. The morning routine included craft making, Bible story-telling and games, just as it had in Henry Berry's day. The evenings were a time to chat informally with teenagers, in the usual Saltshaker fashion. Chat would be followed by a short talk from a leader. For Louise, individual children 'stood out' in these summer schemes, such as a young girl called Mary, who was happy, positive and mature for her years. Unfortunately Mary would face tragedy in the months to come.

Louise stresses that the tone was still evangelistic. It focused on the supreme value of a faith in Christ. There was also a mildly evangelistic dimension to the special 'summer scheme service' held in the Duncairn church on the final Sunday of the project, to which all the young people, their family and friends were invited.

Louise remembers how difficult it was as a Protestant teenager to feel wholly at ease within the culture of this Nationalist neighbourhood. Personal names were invariably Gaelic in origin and the Catholic imagery of Christ's cross was a popular element in the girls' jewelry -

'In the church entrance hall, registration time seemed noisy and busy. There were up to fifty kids. The youngest were aged 3 or 4. I was on the registration table on the first day, taking the children's names and addresses. I had to move because I was having difficulty spelling "Irish" names and the youngest were too little to tell me how names such as Aoife and Siobhan were spelt. They did recognize if I spelt it wrongly but were unable to tell me how to make it right! This made me feel very Protestant! I did own a gold chain with a small cross on it and I can remember wearing it during the summer scheme and feeling that it helped me fit in!'

The attitude of most New Lodge families was still positive and polite as it had been in earlier days. Louise feels that the workers at the 174 Trust were still perceived as 'Christians', rather than 'Ulster Protestants'. She thinks the work at 174 was respected by the wider community because when the minibus had its windows broken by vandals, there was 'real anger at whoever had done it.'

For Louise, the summer scheme was a 'rite of passage' into adulthood. She liked the way the team would 'hang out' and chat on the grass at the side entrance to the church, enjoying the sun –

'I suppose I was quite impressed by myself! I enjoyed the challenge to be involved in work so close to my home yet in a world which was a million times removed from me. I enjoyed the "craic" each night after the young people had gone and then eating a Chinese carry-out at Patton's house to celebrate the end of the scheme.'

However some grim memories have surfaced for Louise, many years later:

'One night some local young people climbed up onto the roof of the church and threw bottles and eggs at anyone leaving the halls. It was an unnerving few hours as we could hear them running on the roof above where we were. I have no idea how it was resolved but eventually they stopped and went away.'[91]

If I get off my spiritual pedestal

Meanwhile Dave Moser was facing the challenges of sustained commitment to North Belfast. He was forced to say in a letter home that:

'The thing I find most discouraging here are the Christians who drive to church on Sundays, sit like bumps, drive home and never once let God's love and grace produce any by-products like sharing, caring and service.'

And he despaired of the conformity and distrust of difference, lamenting what he saw as:

'the tug and pull in Northern culture of questioning and doubting others. When prejudice is based on religious foundations, all variations soon become questionable.'

Yet perhaps Dave failed to see the degree to which Christian vibrancy and openness had been steadily eroded within a community that felt itself to have been under 'terrorist' attack for many years and in which many people also felt they had been subject to betrayal by an uncaring British establishment.

Dave deeply admired those Protestants who had a valid personal faith but also recognised their social responsibilities. He thought of Jeff who had recently arrived as a volunteer. Jeff had been appalled to witness a new church spire erected at some expense in his home village in County Down and decided to leave his paid work to do a year's voluntary Christian service. Now he was coping with 'the lads' of the New Lodge, four of whom had got into trouble again, 'scooped' for going up to the army guard post and swinging on the outside gate until it fell off.

One other feature of the lifestyle of some New Lodge lads was their increased use of drugs. One Saltshaker regular recalls smoking 'dope' on the premises although he was never caught. Some lads were experimenting at home with 'acid' and others with 'e-tabs' although the mellow or hallucinatory euphoria induced by some of these substances was scarcely of help to the implementation of an 'armed struggle.' Inevitably, several locals did get involved with the lucrative drugs trade and paid a cost in terms of community disapproval, severe IRA disciplinary proceedings or a spell behind bars.[92]

Dave Moser had a chance to gain insight into the life behind bars when he went with one young man to visit his brother who was incarcerated at the prison in Long Kesh, having confessed to a killing in 1981. Dave noted how his friend carried a secret note to his brother, which was contained in a tiny cellophane package within his mouth.

When his friend's brother had arrived at the gaol he had been placed in a cell whose walls were still encrusted with dried excrement from the 'dirty protest' that had preceded the hunger strikes, in which Republican prisoners had smeared their walls with their own waste rather than 'slop out' as 'criminals' were supposed to do.

This young man had studied in gaol, gaining qualifications in theology. He had also written poetry. Dave returned from Long Kesh to the 174 Trust, determined to keep in touch with him. He started sending books by Mennonite authors who argued that the practice of pacifism was the only way to avoid causing further injustice when responding to hurts and wrongs.

Dave was troubled by some workers at the trust who espoused Ulster's more strident brands of faith, in which they had their theology 'all figured out' and saw the Saltshaker as a simple, no-nonsense attempt to 'convert' young Nationalists. He was perturbed by the way that training sessions for the staff often excluded the 'non-Christian' workers. Partly because they were marginalized in this way, he was inclined to feel more intimacy with these 'unbelievers' than with theologically over-confident members of the 174 staff who were theoretically his Christian brothers and sisters.

What kept Dave going was the honesty and vigour of the 174 clientele. He recorded in his diary:

'As I get close to the lads I see more of their fears and pain in one week than I have seen in a year of 174 community meetings.'

And despite the sorrow of seeing many of these boys' earlier faith commitments melt away, he kept writing home to Indiana and telling his family:

'I pray that they will understand and accept the truth of Christ.'

The trial and sentencing of the rioters was still postponed. Dave took some of them to Dublin to meet a youth group from one of the more disadvantaged areas of the Irish capital, only to be amazed by how little the young people from the two parts of Ireland had in common, despite the desire for Irish unity amongst the Saltshaker regulars.

With the younger age-group, there was considerable success in the perennial 174 challenge of bringing the New Lodge and Tiger's Bay together. In the 1989 summer scheme, Dave counted numerous Protestant participants among the 130 who were gathered at the trust.

And while the tense wait for the trials continued, Dave was amazed at the talents of some of the local men. One young man called Jim Corry was a talented singer and his acting skills soon became apparent too. Through his contacts with a 174 worker called Dave Calvert, who had had a lot of theatre experience, Jim became involved in drama, auditioned for several roles in theatre and TV work and actually played the role of a British soldier in one particular film! Jim was a regular at the Saltshaker café where he enjoyed an 'Ulster Fry' and a 'mug of splosh'. He often entertained students with special needs at an education centre on the Crumlin Road, teaching them 'the basics of music'. [93]

Meanwhile, Dave Moser's letters home contained a gallery of local characters. That gallery included Bob the caretaker at the Duncairn Church. Everyone in the area knew that Bob was an Orangeman, who walked out of the house in his suit and tie with his boots polished on the 12th of July, heading for the annual parade. Yet, despite some taunting and opposition, he remained within his house on Thorndale Avenue throughout the 'Troubles'.

Bob was distressed at seeing the local children playing in the grounds of the church, climbing trees and causing damage to property. He berated the culprits and was called an 'ould Orange bastard' for his trouble. Dave tried to mediate between Bob and the children, with a measure of success.

As the first months of 1990 passed, there was little reason for fresh optimism in Dave Moser's mind. He noted with weariness that 'the first sectarian taunts of Spring' were being shouted across the local park. He looked at the 174 Trust's chairman and saw in Patton's face the signs of deep exhaustion, caused by tensions within the organisation and also the daily challenges of being immersed in his embattled North Belfast pastorate.

> 'Patton describes himself as a sponge that cannot take any more hurt' - wrote Dave in one of his weekly letters home.[94]

Indeed the tensions that Patton faced were massive. Even the time-limited summer scheme projects were a source of pain. Some of his congregation were far from happy at New Lodge children colonizing their church premises for the summer. A few Mennonite volunteers from abroad took exception to the evangelistic tone of some of the 174 Trust's work, seeing it as inappropriate in a divided society.

Patton struggled at times with the values of his full-time volunteers. Dave Moser's pacifist traditions were a problem. Patton felt that his Mennonite stance inclined Dave to an inflexible bias against the British Army because they were clad in military uniform and holding guns.

And then there were the rebuffs Patton received when trying to help the young men of the neighbourhood. He went to court to give a favourable reference for a lad who had been 'lifted' for riotous behavior, including possession of petrol bombs. As a result, the young man got off with a spell of community service whereas his mates ended up behind bars. Rather than feeling grateful, the young man was furious that he had not been able to suffer for the cause, like his friends! [95]

Dave too was feeling exhausted. He was doing a 70 hour week and finding little time to nourish the relationship with Beth. At least there was consolation in the innocence of the little girls from the neighbourhood, who turned up at the door of the Moser house and asked if Beth would come out to play with them or make them some 'cookies.'

To Dave it was little wonder that the young men of the area often resorted to drink as a way of dealing with the extremity of their surroundings. When one lad received £8,000 compensation for being wrongfully shot in an incident involving the army, he immediately purchased a stash of 'booze' and shared it with his friends. On that particular Tuesday night, the Christian musician Kenny Duncan was performing in the Saltshaker and the drinkers caused disturbance by congregating outside. Dave found out that 15 of the lads had consumed 96 tins of beer, 20 bottles of cider and 6 bottles of spirits amongst them.

Dave also had to deal with the presence of alcohol stowed away on the minibus that took the young people on outings on sunny summer evenings. On one evening, the 174 bus travelled to the rocky inlet of Portmuck, followed by a visit to the strand at Brown's Bay, at the far end of the scenic peninsula known as Islandmagee. As some of the boys lay on the beach, gazing at the sea, out came the cider. Later, as the driver headed for home along the winding coastal roads, a cry was heard from the back of the bus:

'Kevin is throwing up'.

As Dave went to a nearby farmhouse to get warm water and a cloth to clean up Kevin's mess, some of the young people 'introduced themselves' to the cattle in the nearby fields.

At times like this, Dave wondered why he bothered.

However, he kept on trying to get the New Lodge lads away to America for a 'break' on a scheme for which the late Billy Kane had once been a candidate. 'Tanzy' Campbell and Pat Grogan both availed of the offer and spent several months working in Indiana and Ohio.[96] For Pat this was a scary experience as he had never travelled far before. On the plane to New York he got intoxicated on the contents of the in-flight drinks trolley and by the time he arrived at Blufton, Ohio to stay with his Christian hosts, he was badly hungover.

Once installed in Blufton, Pat went to a local college to study art and worked in a nearby lumber mill to finance his studies. The self-sufficient Mennonite family with whom he resided, sent him to pick corn from the fields for the next day's meals and they introduced him to their friends, including one old lady who asked if he spoke English. Pat was unable to stay the full term, homesick for the familiarities of Belfast.[97]

As for other 'kids' who would never get away to the USA, a cycle ride along the towpath of the Lagan canal on the outskirts of the city often proved beneficial. Dave and 'Tanzy' offered to take a group of New Lodge youngsters on this trip, if they possessed a bike. The ride along this sylvan 18th century waterway was a totally new experience for most of the participants.

Beth and Dave were now determined on going back to America to undertake further training, Beth to study for qualifications in health education and Dave to prepare for training in full-time Christian ministry. As the time for departure from Northern Ireland grew nearer, Dave found solace in regular bike rides into the Irish countryside and walks to the top of Cavehill.

And despite the traumas and disappointments of the period he had spent at the Saltshaker, Dave now knew who Christ would have identified with in today's world:

'I have learned that Christ is on the side of the unemployed, the misunderstood, the mistreated, the down and out, the depressed. By listening to others, I earn the right to share what I know. If I get off my spiritual pedestal, I can share my spiritual life with others on equal ground.'

Unfortunately, during the last few months at the trust, Dave had one of his worst experiences since coming to Northern Ireland. He was the joint leader for an expedition to the outdoor SHARE centre in County Fermanagh. This trip involved some 174 regulars and a few members of the Hob youth club in Holywood.

By 10-30pm on the Saturday of the visit, many of the young people were drunk and disorderly. They were ordered off the site by the centre manager and Dave spent several night-time hours looking for petrol in Enniskillen, to fuel the bus journey back to Belfast. Eventually they arrived home at 6-30 on Sunday morning. The bus disgorged its load of 'hungover' and chastened teenagers.

But as the departure date loomed, both Dave and Beth were focused on good memories of their Irish adventure as well as the dark aspects. Beth wrote home to her family to say:

'I feel extremely sad leaving what has become my home. It is a sensory delight to go through the countryside on bicycle or on foot and find the peace that nature always seems to bring to me. But you can almost feel the gloom of mourning and famine on some rainy days….this place reeks of history…'

Beth and Dave were aware that human enmity was not just a local phenomenon. As citizens of the United States, they worried about the Gulf War which was looming ever since Saddam Hussein invaded Kuwait. American and British troops were on their way to the Middle East, confident of quick success, a move that prompted the New Lodge gable-end graffito:

'Gone to the Gulf – back in two weeks…' [98]

The Gulf War was not Dave's only cause of worry about USA foreign policy. On one occasion Bill Fleming heard him read out a letter from a Mennonite friend in Nicaragua, which described in critical language the behavior of the Contras who had opposed the Socialist regime in that country and whom President Reagan had described as 'Freedom Fighters.' [99]

In September 1990, Dave completed a sponsored cycling trip around Ulster, which raised £600 for youth work at the Saltshaker. It was a fitting way to end three years in Ulster, as Dave had grown to love the countryside which he had cycled through so often. He had developed a love for gazing up at the cliffs of Cave Hill, which were a constant presence above North Belfast. Dave got to know the local saying:

'If you can't see Cave Hill, it's raining and if you can see it then it's about to rain.' [100]

And he enjoyed Alice Milligan's poetic injunction:

'Look up from the streets of the city,
Look high beyond tower and mast.
What hand of what Titan sculptor
Smote the crags on the mountain vast?' [101]

A few days after Dave's last bike-ride, the Mosers left Ireland to return to the States.

Taking the soup?

During Derek McCorkell's tenure of the directorship, a fresh generation of volunteers came and went. One new person was Kerry Nicholson who had travelled from County Waterford in the south-east of the Irish Republic, where he had grown up in a family of 'mixed religion'. Raised as a Catholic, he attended a Quaker school, after which he went to Art College in Limerick in 1986, when he started to involve himself in a small Christian Union group and attended a Protestant Church in the town.

At the conclusion of his art studies, Kerry undertook teacher-training but found it uncongenial and at this stage he became aware of Careforce, the organization which offered Christians an opportunity for voluntary engagement in areas of social need. A position caught Kerry's eye in 1991, involving work which was to be jointly undertaken at the 174 Trust and the Duncairn Presbyterian Church.

He was unfamiliar with Belfast. He had rarely been north of a line stretching between Dublin and Galway. However in July 1991, he had a chance to find out about the work that would begin in earnest that autumn. He stayed for a few days with the team who were operating the 174 summer scheme on the lower Antrim Road.

Kerry recalls his first night in Belfast when he bedded down in the Thomas Sinclair Memorial Hall. He was there with many other young people, including a team from the University Presbyterian Church in Seattle. Amongst the group were several 174 Trust 'locals' who had been drafted in as 'minders'. In the middle of the night eerie noises came from the roof. The 'minders' told Kerry that this was IRA men trying to gain access to the building. He was in no position to grasp that this was a joke.[102]

(Such practical jokes were by now a part of the 'induction process' for new volunteers at the 174 Trust. On one occasion, at the trust's house on the Cliftonville Road, a bunch of Saltshaker regulars entered the premises, wearing the sinister-looking balaclava helmets often used by the IRA. They 'held up' the new inmates, much to their consternation. The team of 'pretend-terrorists' had been aided and abetted by Dave Maley, who by this stage had become an enthusiastic convert to North Belfast's black humour. The 'gunmen' certainly relished their 'joke' as they had acquired life-like replica guns as well as luxurious silk balaclavas, sewn together by devoted female relatives.)[103]

Despite his rude introduction to New Lodge humour, Kerry began a period of full-time volunteering in September. He started as a youth worker but moved towards responsibility for administrative and journalistic tasks, including production of the Saltshaker newspaper, which kept the project's supporters, far and wide, informed about the work. At this stage, Kerry lived in the attic at the top of the 174 premises. He spent a lot of the time in the 174 office which was now on the first floor, above the café.

Derek McCorkell continued the policy of mentoring young people from the district who were going through personal difficulties and he offered them accommodation at the trust, or in his own house. So Kerry soon got to know his new 174 neighbours.

However, Kerry was having difficulty combining his 174 duties with his promised commitment to the Duncairn church. As someone raised in a Waterford Catholic environment, he found the Duncairn church very 'British', very dark and awfully forbidding. Taking refuge in the McCorkell household, he decided to leave the constraints of his Careforce job behind and applied for an ACE grant, enabling him to train for a course in 'community management'. Eventually he did return to the 174 Trust and lived above the Saltshaker, volunteering for daily work there whilst undertaking his new training course.

He grew to enjoy life in the flat above the café. He liked the company of Tonia Davidson, a volunteer from Seattle, who resided on the premises. Roberta and Margaret, who ran the café, prepared good food which Kerry availed of on a daily basis. Bowls of stew, curry and rice, plates of freshly made chips and a variety of desserts all made an appearance. At this stage, not only was there a regular early morning prayer meeting at the trust but also a lunchtime worship session once a week. The handful of locals who had made a 'profession of faith' would come along.

The famous BBC TV program 'Songs of Praise' paid a visit to the trust during Kerry's stay in Belfast. To his surprise, he ended up showing a TV presenter the city's infamous 'peace walls', erected to keep warring factions apart. For all his recent arrival in the city, Kerry felt he knew North Belfast quite well.

But this was still an intimidating place to live, although the conflict was inching towards political resolution. The infamous Girdwood army watchtower, which had recently been adorned with the slogan 'DON'T FEED THE MONKEYS', had now been pulled down. But Kerry found the presence of the military forces unnerving.

On several occasions he was stopped and searched by soldiers as he walked along the street. This induced feelings of violation. There was a danger of 'drive-by' shootings by Loyalist militants, for whom Kerry would have been deemed an anonymous but 'legitimate' target in their war with communities that 'harboured' the IRA.

A different problem was presented by the intense argumentation of some Saltshaker clients. Arguments with one young man in the café focused on how Kerry as a 'southerner', was a citizen of an Irish Republic which had 'let the people of the New Lodge down'. This young man believed that the northern Catholics had been left to languish as Ulster's 'second-class citizens'. He regretted that the IRA's 'armed struggle' had been denounced by the Irish government.

However Kerry had grown up in the Irish Republic during the 1980s and his country had been economically stagnant. Many of its talented young people had to emigrate to find work. The North seemed to have many benefits denied to the South, including ready access to grants and an improving housing stock, as evidenced by scores of new homes built in the New Lodge. North Belfast still had terrible deprivation, of course. So too did vast swathes of the southern Irish society with which New Lodge Republicans wanted to be united.

One feature of Kerry's upstairs flat was its elevated viewpoint. Out of the back windows of the Saltshaker flat there was an evening vista of sunset behind the dark edge of the Belfast Hills. Out of the front windows there was an extensive view over the inner-city rooftops and down towards the waters of Belfast Lough. On several occasions Kerry was awakened by the throb of helicopter blades and he would go to the window to watch a 'chopper' directing an intense searchlight beam onto one of the New Lodge tower-blocks where an army raid was taking place. The sound of gunfire was sometimes heard in nearby streets.

On other occasions, Protestant parades were to be seen, as band-members went marching down the Cliftonville Road to the sound of drums, flutes and accordions, on the other side of enormous screens erected by the army to keep a barrier between marchers and adjacent New Lodge residents.

On one occasion, a hijacked bus burned fiercely on the road outside the flat during a Republican protest against some recent injustice. Kerry and his flat-mates had to move away from the windows to avoid the heat. Later the bus's tyres could be heard exploding in the conflagration.

By 1993, Kerry had found a job in the more peaceful seaside town of Newcastle, working for Age Concern. He had also met Karen, his future partner. But before he left the New Lodge, he had become aware of one particular feature of 174 that seemed problematic. Catholics had been employed by the 174 Trust and some had resided on the premises but very few made it onto the management team. Kerry only knew of one such person and he was a Liverpudlian who had come from England to marry a local girl.[104]

Arguably, what Kerry noticed was that the 174 Trust had unwittingly reproduced old patterns of employment inherited from Ireland's colonial past. Any reliable Irish history book would show that in bygone years Protestants throughout the island owned much of the property and many of the wealthiest businesses. Poor Catholics often had to come, cap-in-hand, looking for work. What is more, at various times throughout Irish history, pressure had been put by Protestants on impoverished or starving Catholics to 'change their religion', thereby gaining crucial material benefit.

Tony Macaulay's quip about 'ACE' Christians was appropriate. During the catastrophic Irish Potato Famine in the mid-19th century, the term 'soupers' had been coined for starving Catholics who were 'taking the soup' offered by several Protestant famine relief agencies, on condition that they accept the 'Reformation Faith'. Did Kerry Nicholson sense that the methodology of the 174 Trust could trigger communal memories such as these? Was the 174's attempt to found a cross-community Christian project, dedicated to a pure 'New Testament gospel', going to be darkened by the shadow of ancient grievances?[105]

And how truly 'cross-community' was a project that prided itself on its cross-community status, if it was merely run by Protestants for inhabitants of a Catholic area?

However, to young men like Ricky Allen, such issues of institutional balance within 174 were of little relevance. When he was in his mid-teens, Ricky had been hit in the face by a missile, thrown at Duncairn Gardens . He had been visiting his father who, at that stage lived near the 'peace-line'. Taken to hospital, he made an initial recovery but then became subject to unpleasant seizures over the next five or six years. He had been planning to go to college to study electronics, having done well in this area of his studies at secondary school. Now that career option had to be abandoned. With a medical condition such as this, no-one could operate safely in such a field of work.

Ricky was in despair. And the trust came to the rescue.

Derek McCorkell was always trying to assist the youth of the New Lodge with practical suggestions for improving their circumstances. If possible he would give them a role at the trust which would get them started in employment and he often encouraged them to further their education or to learn new skills. Josey Grogan and many others had been helped in this way, over the years.

Ricky talked to Derek and he suggested an alternative career route down which he could travel. The Saltshaker director employed him as a trainee youth worker and found funds to help remunerate him whilst he underwent this training.

This was a crucial move. In the next few years, Ricky worked on a community project at St Enoch's church, participated in community drama with a mixed group of disabled and able-bodied young people in East Belfast, obtained a qualification in community work at Queens University and received a commendation for his studies which made him feel 'ten feet tall'. Later he moved on to undertake a diploma in community work, the fees for which he had to find himself, working in a 'burger joint' in the city centre, in order to accumulate the money.

His mother also became involved in 'early years' provision and ran a playgroup on premises belonging to St James's Church of Ireland, further up the Antrim Road, which was a playgroup that eventually moved to the 174 Trust.

Throughout this time, friendships with Saltshaker workers were paramount. In his early years in the café, he had known Dave Moser, who was tall enough to be a basketball player and who seemed to be the quintessential image of an American. Now Ricky was helping to take some of the new American volunteers away on tours of Derry and Donegal in a hired van. They visited prehistoric monuments, walked the empty Atlantic beaches and climbed the windswept hills.

In due course, Ricky met Kelly, who came from the Loyalist area of Highfield and belonged to the Methodist church there. When they first got to know each other, Kelly was searching for a chance to use her skills as an 'early years' childcare worker. Ricky alerted her to a post that was available at the trust. Subsequently Kelly moved on to work in a day nursery in Dunmurry, then after their marriage, Ricky and Kelly moved to Dunmurry to live and Ricky worked in the nursery too. He obtained further qualifications in 'early years' education and eventually the couple began their own nursery business.

Since then Ricky has moved on from 'early years' provision and when he was interviewed in 2009, he was just about to train as a social worker. Meanwhile he has fostered children, been a Dr Barnardo's support worker and a member of the residential staff in a care home run by that organisation. Besides all this he has been a kayak instructor with the Territorial Army and has travelled the world from Alaska to South Africa, providing outdoor training to young servicemen.

When interviewed, Ricky explained that Derek McCorkell and the 174 Trust lay behind all of these changes, having lifted him up when he was languishing in despair as a teenage invalid, in the aftermath of a horrible attack. However, not all of the 174 'package' struck Ricky as being equally worthwhile. He attended Derek's daily prayer meetings at the Saltshaker but wasn't terribly impressed by the devotion he witnessed. Sometimes he thinks that the prayer sessions were merely a management tool to get everyone bonded and focused.

Ricky's disillusion with institutional religion began early. As a youngster he had already decided that he didn't want to be a Catholic altar-boy, as his mother fervently desired. So he rode his BMX bike into St Patrick's Church one day and the priest found him clattering down the altar steps. There was not a chance now of elevation to a role in the sacred rituals of the church, after such impious behaviour.

Ricky was curious to attend various Protestant church services during his 174 years. He sampled a few. In fact he now thinks of himself as a roving anthropologist who studied the huge varieties of worship to be found in Evangelical Belfast. He attended the city's largest church, the plush and busy Metropolitan Tabernacle, where he marveled at its vast auditorium and the throngs of neat Ulster churchgoers, carrying large Bibles.

He was invited to come to a church service in East Belfast by Charles, a disabled man from the New Lodge who was connected to the trust through the PHAB network. Ricky was amazed to see people in the congregation jumping on top of their seats while singing loudly and praising God. Many of them would lift their hands in the air, in a gesture of ecstatic adoration. He heard people cry out and sob and he witnessed the pastor calling in an American accent for 'needy' people to come to the front of the church, where he laid his hands upon them, after which they would fall to the floor in a startled, mystic daze.

At least the worship in the Saltshaker was a little more restrained, with Jim Corry sometimes leading the singing, a small cross dangling from his neck as he played the guitar and sang a handful of well-known worship songs.

Uninhibited Christian worship held no appeal for Ricky but he understood that the people he met at 174 wanted to share such a powerful experience with him. He did not put it down to a malign, sectarian strategy for 'converting him' from Catholicism to Protestantism. It was simply an overwhelming desire to share their main source of happiness in life - a personal faith in Christ.[106]

Freedom dance

A key figure at the 174 Trust in these years was Philip McClean. Like many Saltshaker workers, Philip had grown up as an Ulster Protestant but possessed views that marked him out from many of his peers. Studying Politics and Sociology at Queens University he had become interested in Marxism. Then, on encountering a living Christian faith, he committed himself to the ecumenical 'Community of the King' and spent time living in a household of single Christian men in West Belfast, which included among its members two Catholic priests.

A friend of Philip's in this house had spent time working on a 174 summer scheme and recommended it. Philip contacted Tony Macaulay and he was encouraged to offer his services as a disability volunteer. It would be the start of a decade of commitment.

The 1970s and early 1980s had been a period when a series of 'community care' initiatives was implemented throughout the United Kingdom and many institutions which held people with long-term psychiatric and physical ailments were closed down. Some were placed in flats and apartments where they felt distressed and isolated, especially in an area such as the New Lodge, whose social infrastructure had been so damaged by the conflict. As a result, Philip and his colleagues Deena and Jim Nimick had encountered many people who were in great need of help.

Having begun in the area of disability provision, Philip went on to be the manager of the ACE schemes at 174, as noted earlier in this account. He supervised the move to premises further up the Antrim Road, where the project was renamed as the Community Training and Enterprise Centre. By now the ACE provision had gained immense respect in the New Lodge. No less than half the clients who passed through the doors of the scheme locally were going ahead and finding long-term work.

Then in 1993, when Derek McCorkell left 174 and the organization found itself once more without a director, Patton asked Philip to take on the role of acting manager. As well as the managerial talents that he needed in this role, Philip also possessed a love of creative arts and he was already writing and playing music and beginning to compose fiction.

When interviewed in 2009, Philip still recalled the creativity that characterized the trust in those days. David Calvert, the freelance arts worker, was brought in to run the magazine 'Cromla', which was printed at the Saltshaker and which gave a space to local visual artists and writers. A show called 'Living in Different Worlds' was devised, with much of the script written by Philip. Among the items were songs performed by choirs of Catholic and Protestant school-children. The performance took place at the Old Museum Arts Centre in the heart of the city.

Philip recalls that on a day-by-day basis, anyone might encounter music being performed in the back room of the café, with Jim Corry playing the tin whistle and his friend Keith accompanying him on the guitar. On one occasion the BBC DJ Simon Mayo interviewed the local musicians in an upstairs space at the trust and heard them play. A music group called 'Think Like Fury' was also formed to entertain the children and teenagers during the summer scheme.[107]

Josey Grogan can still recall how the famous traditional musicians, the McPeake family, were brought to the New Lodge to give a concert and how Francie McPeake gave lessons to members of the youth club.

Josey recollects trying to play the tin whistle and the Irish drum known as the bodhran. He can recall the haunting sound of the uillean pipes. At one stage he and his pals were taken to a festival in Lahinch in County Clare, where they participated in music sessions and had a great deal of 'craic'.[108]

The songs from that era still survive on audio tapes. A number were recorded live in the Saltshaker. Some were written by Jim Corry, some by a guitarist called Mark Adair and some by Philip. They speak of the toughness of life on the North Belfast streets and the freedom and love to be found through following Christ. One song spoke in ominous, subdued terms of the overpowering antagonisms of North Belfast:

'The flags they are flying, once a year on this day,
The kerb stones are painted – they've got something to say,
There's a man on the platform, he's got something to say,
I've got a gun in my hand, I've got something to say….'

Another song opened with the line:

'the streets of the city can be a sad affair'

but then went on to speak of the Christian life as a 'freedom dance' and invited the listeners to 'leave their burdens behind' and follow Christ. Perhaps the most powerful song was the one that American volunteer Chris Rogers had heard sung in the open air at the close of a 174 summer-scheme. It proclaimed a desire to seek God's help in replacing hate with love:

'Lord, I know it's hard but for this place it must be done
And Lord I know no peace can come by a bomb or a gun,
And Lord you know the days I've smiled and the nights I've cried,
But Lord you know I'm true because I love you deep inside.

Lord, I'm tired of seeing my friends taken away,
And Lord I just want to live in peace from day to day,
And Lord give me love in my heart,
Take my hatred away,

Lord give me patience and strength to live for you each day
And Lord my God, give me light in my life to lead a better way…' [109]

This is a complicated journey

Tonia Davidson, who had come as a volunteer to Belfast from the USA, was also a witness to the work of the trust at this time when Belfast was standing on the verge of change. She came to live in the Saltshaker flat with its vistas of the Antrim Road on one side and the Antrim Hills on the other.

'I remember the first night that I met the younger club (9-12 year olds) in the church halls of Duncairn Presbyterian church. Four boys in tracksuits burst through the front door, ran down the hall, grabbed snooker sticks off a felt table and began fighting each other, kung-fu style. I tried bringing order to this bunch of lads with very little success. Thankfully, along came Alex Tennant to the 174 Trust. She not only became a dear friend but an invaluable co-worker. Gradually we brought structure to the club, which the kung-fu boys didn't like - and they eventually left. In my discouragement over this, Alex reminded me that by creating a safe environment, other children might attend who otherwise wouldn't, for fear of the chaos. She was right.

First, came bright-eyed Patrick. He showed up the next week with his fiery friend, John Joe. Then they brought two other friends, whom they affectionately called Big Barry and Little Barry. After their arrival, many other children began attending: Patrick's cousins, John Joe's big sister and many more from the neighborhood. These four boys made up the core of the new club and they always played a dynamic role in leading the group.

In thinking about this club, two memories stand out. First was the night we talked about The Good Samaritan. When I asked "Who is your neighbour?", eager Big Barry pointed to his friend:

"Ach, Paddy he's my neighbor, so he is. He lives closest to me, closer than John Joe."

Mary was Patrick's cousin. She gave Big Barry a nudge and declared :

"She's talking about everyone being our neighbours, even those living in Tiger's Bay."

Mary's answer surprised me. The kids usually described the Loyalist people living in Tiger's Bay in such exaggerated terms that they didn't sound human. After a litany of protests as to why those in Tiger's Bay couldn't be their neighbours, Patrick - who I could always count on to be level-headed, spoke:

"My Ma says we're supposed to forgive because it's good for us, not just them. Is that what you mean about them being our neighbours?"

It wasn't. But it was a helpful answer. Then John Joe ended our discussion by saying

"I'll forgive you, Tonia, if you let us get back to playing our games."

And so we returned to playing a club favorite, dodgeball.

Sadly, nine months after that discussion, Mary's dad was shot dead in front of her house. I saw her only once after that. I'll always remember the way she gathered up the other children, tending to them in kind ways. She was definitely mature beyond her years. I hope that that maturity and wisdom helped her through the tragic loss of her father. I can only pray that it has.

One other memory is of climbing Slieve Donard in the Mourne Mountains with this group. The leaders were Jamie - who was another youth worker - Alex and myself. We were determined to reach the top, even in the unexpected hailstorm. Later, Alex and Jamie told me I was the driving force in reaching the peak, but in reality, one word from them and I would've turned back. I actually took my lead from the kids.

While taking a break, we sat huddled against the man-made Mourne Wall which strides over the peaks on this mountain range, in order to shelter ourselves from the wind. The cloud-covered summit loomed above us. We were discouraged that after all our efforts we were still a couple of hundred feet from our goal. Then, all of a sudden, Patrick and John Joe sprang ahead and encouraged us to move forward. Which we did! Big Barry was terrified. Mary and a few others gathered around him, promising to walk with him to the top. Being linked arm and arm with his friends gave Barry the courage he needed to leave the shelter of the rock wall. After a hard struggle against the wind, we eventually made it to the top. At the peak, the kids found energy to climb in and out of the cairn at the summit. Their faces beamed with satisfaction.

When we finally descended, it couldn't have been more like a dramatic movie moment. In perfect timing, the clouds parted, revealing to us, for the first time, a view of Newcastle and the coastline. We could even see our little camp of orange tents, lying to the west. As we let the steep slope pull us downward, half stumbling, half walking down the mountainside, the children started singing a praise song. I'm not sure who began singing but they all knew the song. It wasn't one that we sang in club. I wish I could remember the exact words. But I do remember thinking at the time how fitting the words were—declaring the beauty and majesty of God's creation.

When I was later instructed to steer these children towards the neighborhood Protestant church, I was shocked. These children had faith - one that was being nurtured by the Catholic Church. Also, considering the political climate at the time, it seemed like a ridiculous, if not dangerous request to make of these children—to walk past their family and neighbors on a Sunday morning and through the doors of a Protestant church. I think the mid-week clubs offered by the trust were the best way that we could contribute to meeting the spiritual and emotional needs of these children.

There was another group that had a great influence on my time at the 174 Trust. This was a bunch of young men, whom I found spending much of their time drinking in front of the Saltshaker. During my first few months, I heard many of their personal stories, coupled with Irish history. This was partly because, in one sense, their favourite game was - "Scare the American". But it also seemed like they had a sense of duty to share their tragic tales of British oppression with an outsider. Maybe they thought it would somehow bring help to their situation.

One of these men I shall call Seamus.

Seamus was a dramatic storyteller. His language painted a vivid picture of Irish history. He described the Atlantic as a gigantic graveyard due to massive emigration to America where Catholics sought freedom from oppressive British landlords. He also dwelt on the burning of Catholic homes during the early years of the Troubles in the 1960's and 1970's. He spoke of his experience as a young boy, when he watched his father being taken away to be imprisoned during the period when Republican suspects were interned without trial. His stories touched a part of me that is fiercely protective of those who have been mistreated. I was angry.

It was in listening to Seamus and the stories told by the other lads that I began to question what the difference is between war and terrorism. I reflected on my own country's independence. I had never thought of our 18th century Revolutionary War as made up of 'terrorist' acts. I began to ponder: when is violence justified? Could the Irish Republican cause be an act of war rather than terrorism?

But it was at the height of this questioning, that I also saw how men like Seamus remained stuck in 'victimhood' thinking. The constant replaying of history, without talk of forgiveness, made me wonder if this mental state was more 'prison-like' than anything their ancestors had experienced. When I realized this, it brought me back to my original mission in coming to Ireland —talking about the forgiveness represented by Christ's cross.

This may sound hardhearted, coming from a woman who hasn't endured a violent history. But it was through my care for these men that I began to understand the significance of forgiveness, not only in reconciling us to God, but in its empowerment to free us from any human conflict. Forgiveness doesn't erase the physical acts of violence but it seems to be the porthole to redemption.

Where there is conflict, there is opportunity for mercy. I'm interested in being with people in those moments where they - even in unfathomable circumstances - extend forgiveness. Forgiveness in its mysterious way brings freedom. Just as young Patrick had once shared with me - forgiveness may be more for us who forgive than for those on the receiving end. At least that's a starting point - even if it is appealing to our selfish nature - when forgiveness feels like the most unnatural thing to do.

I'm not sure what happened to Seamus. While I was there he was drawn back into paramilitary activity. When I left, he was awaiting trial. I pray that wherever he is, he experiences freedom.

Roberta and Margaret, the sisters who ran the café, are iconic to me of the Saltshaker. Dressed in her red café uniform, Roberta welcomed customers into the cafe with her frank yet friendly manner. She knew something about everyone, which helped her to make people feel at home. During our staff meetings, Margaret talked about Jesus in such a personal manner that I felt I could almost see him standing in our midst. These experiences were important to me as a young woman who was new in my faith - seeing how faith was worked out in hospitality, truth-speaking and intimacy with Jesus.

Many times I was struck by the communal spirit of the people living in the New Lodge, even in the smallest of gestures. For example, with the older youth club (13-17 year olds) we would often take a break and run over to the 'sweetie' shop. Instantly, wrappers were opened and the sweets passed around. Selfishly, I'd look at my tube of Smarties, sneak a few and then reluctantly offer some to the kids. Each time we entered the sweet shop, with my mouth watering for candy-coated chocolate, it never occurred to me that I'd be sharing the treats I bought. Yet, without fail, even before tasting their own candy, these teenagers passed their sweets around to their mates. What kind of youth worker would I be, if I didn't share? One day a Smartie tube was left on my desk—most likely a gift from this youth club.

Life in the flat above the Saltshaker was a big part of my experience at the 174 Trust. When I first arrived, a lad whom I shall call Paul and another former summer scheme youth whom I shall call Ronan, lived in the flat and were employed by the trust as 'ACE' workers. Both were a big help with the youth clubs. Paul, a charismatic figure, captured the children's attention with his zeal for his new found faith. Ronan also looked up to Paul like a big brother. Another volunteer, a recent university graduate from the south of Ireland, called Kerry, and the director's niece, Ursula, who worked in the café, also lived in the flat. Shortly after my arrival, a friend of Paul's, named Mick, joined us.

The place was full, which was helpful during my initial period of culture shock and homesickness. There was always someone in the front room to talk with. Usually Mick sat on the couch smoking cigarettes, careful not to reveal too much of himself. His reserve was the very opposite of Paul's eagerness to share stories. Every evening at 6:00pm, Kerry ate apples and cheese while watching the nightly news. Ursula, somewhere in the background, barked orders on how to keep a tidier flat. And Ronan followed Paul, trying to find his place in the world.

It was in this atmosphere that I entered the 174 Trust. I remember one evening trying to delicately suggest that we remove one of Paul's Republican paintings from the front room. I chose Thanksgiving Day, hoping he might be sympathetic to my decorating ideas, since it was an American holiday and I was so far from home. I thought this approach might work better than telling him his pictures scared me. I was sensitive to the fact that he had painted the pictures himself. And I even admired this about him. But nonetheless the pictures were disturbing and they were more appropriate subject matter for wall murals, like the many he had painted in the neighborhood.

"Ach, we can't put your poster there. Then I'd have to move this picture." Paul pointed to the picture of an IRA man wearing a balaclava.

"Why do you need to put that up? We have plenty of pictures on the walls, so we do."

Kerry glanced away from the evening newscast -

"Paul, why don't you ask what she likes about her picture?"

"Ach, I don't need a man from the south telling me what to put on my walls."

"Paul, I'm Irish. I'm not the enemy. Anyway for Tonia's sake ask her why she wants her picture on the wall."

Paul started to reply but I cut in:

"because I like to look at something that relaxes me and can transport me somewhere else."

"These don't transport you?"

Paul pointed to the Irish Republican tricolours and freedom slogans around the room.

"No, it's like looking out the window."

Mick laughed.

"She's got a point, Paul"

Later that evening they surprised me by rearranging the front room for a Thanksgiving meal. With the couches pushed aside, they placed one of the café tables into the middle of the room. This allowed all of us to sit down together for a traditional Thanksgiving dinner, something they knew was important to me.

These evenings together in the flat gave me hope that the light of Christ was transforming these men—Mick, Paul and Ronan. I'm not sure what exactly gave me hope but there was something in our family-like interactions that sparked this hope. I can see now how important this hope was for me.

Little did I know how much things were about to change from that Thanksgiving meal. Kerry left for a holiday. Ursula moved back to England. And the front room was transformed into a den filled with the men who met with Mick and Paul in the evenings. These men gathered around a table, talking amongst themselves. The dark room, lit by only a table lamp, was an eerie contrast to the season outside, with its cheery Christmas decorations.

Then on Christmas Day, Mick and Paul disappeared. They were arrested in January. Around this time Ronan returned to his home down the street. Shortly after this, I began 'wrestling' with God. When things had not turned out as I expected with those three lads, it somehow became a valve, allowing the pain and suffering of the area to seep through and overwhelm me. I still believed that putting our trust in Jesus would totally realign our lives. But I was beginning to see that this is a long and complicated journey. Out of these wrestlings, my faith continues to grow. It has become less dependent on what is seen and based more in the understanding that God is with us.

As I've continued to sit with people in pain, in my job as a counsellor and family therapist, I've come to appreciate this 'companionship' quality of God.

By the following Christmas, the flat was a very different place. Kerry still lived there. Alex had joined us, as well as another American volunteer from my church, called Sarah. Dinner parties were a regular form of entertainment with other 174 Trust workers and friends from throughout Belfast. In December Kerry cheered the dingy front room with Christmas decorations. In the evenings during that winter month, at the same table in the corner under a lone lamp, Alex lovingly painted Christmas cards for each of her friends.

As an outsider to Northern Ireland, it's hard to separate my specific experience at the 174 Trust from my shock at entering a war zone. You could always tell how new someone was to Belfast by how much they noticed the signs of war—razor wire, helicopters hovering overhead, British patrols dressed in urban camouflage manouvering through the neighbourhoods, heavily patrolled check-points and armoured Land Rovers. While these details were foreground to newcomers, it was surprising how these details faded into normalcy for those from Belfast.

Even though these signs of war eventually faded to the background for me, their effects crept into daily life when I returned to the States. For at least five years after returning to Seattle, I flinched every time a helicopter flew overhead. And whenever I heard about violence in Northern Ireland, I would quickly scan the newspapers for names, hoping not to recognize any of them.

As time has passed it's the memories of relationships that surface first, with the signs of war fading into the background. I no longer flinch when helicopters fly overhead. It has also been a while since I've read about Northern Ireland in the newspaper. I take that as a good sign—the signs of war fading into history.' [110]

May earth rest lightly over you

During the early 1990s, a number of 174 volunteers experienced loss. Having moved to Akron, Pennsylvania, to live, Dave and Beth Moser would enjoy just nine more months of married life. On 26th August 1991, Beth was working in the Diamond Station Store in Ephrata, where she was making money to help with her studies in health education. A customer found her lying lifeless on the shop floor, shortly before 8pm. She never regained consciousness. Beth was just 31.

Tony and Lesley Macaulay flew to the States to be a part of the funeral and to represent the trust. The service was held at the Akron Mennonite Church and Beth's family requested that as a memorial gesture, contributions should be made to the Mennonite Ireland Missions program. Dave came back to Belfast to take part in an emotional but deeply reaffirming memorial service for Beth in a packed Thomas Sinclair Hall. The cause of Beth's premature death was now known to be acute cardiac failure.

The night of Beth's service in the New Lodge was cold and dark and there was tension on the streets due to a recent upsurge in violence. However a wide range of friends turned up and many took part. Tony and Lesley Macaulay read an Irish Blessing which concluded with the words:

> 'May earth rest so lightly over you that your spirit
> May be out from under it quickly and up, and off,
> And on its way to God.' [111]

At lunchtime on 23rd October, 1993, unforeseen tragedy struck another couple who had been involved with the 174 Trust. Alan McBride's wife

Sharon, who had contributed on many occasions to the local youth work, was helping out in her father's fish shop on the Shankill Road. Two men, dressed in white coats and posing as delivery men, arrived at the shop with a tray containing a covered dish, in which was hidden a bomb timed with a short fuse.

IRA operatives in Belfast had seemingly thought that a key meeting of the local leaders of a Loyalist militia, the Ulster Defence Association, was taking place in a room adjacent to the shop. However, any plans that the IRA men may have had to give a warning - allowing swift evacuation of the shop before the bomb went off - were rendered irrelevant when the device exploded prematurely, demolishing the building in an instant.

No UDA meeting was being held next to the shop. All the Shankill Road victims were uninvolved civilians.

Local people and rescue services scrambled through the rubble. They tried to retrieve the bodies of those who had been inside the fish-shop. It was clear that death and injury had occurred on a terrible scale. Alan, on hearing that there had been an explosion on the Shankill, hurried to the scene:

'As soon as I turned the corner and saw the shop I knew there was no-one getting out of there alive. I went crazy, shouting and crying.'

Then, on arriving at the hospital to which the remains of the victims had been taken, Alan discovered the accident and emergency area to be:

'like the waiting-room of hell. There were families in every corner of the room. They were waiting in line to be told their loved ones were dead. We were last in line and weren't told until about 5pm. Nothing can prepare you for being told your wife is dead. I just went crazy.'

Not only was Sharon dead but so too was her father. He was well-known throughout North Belfast's Evangelical circles as a gospel-singer. Among the other Shankill people killed in the bomb were a seven year old schoolgirl and her parents. One of the bombers, Thomas Begley, also died in the blast. That night, Alan had to begin the task of explaining to his two year old daughter Zoe that her mother and her grandfather would not be 'coming back'. [112]

Sharon's funeral at Antrim Road Baptist church was the only ceremony connected to the Shankill bomb which was held in a Catholic area. Henry Davis recalls the day vividly and remembers that the road outside the church was packed with local people who wanted to show their respects.[113]

The kind of trauma caused by the Shankill bomb was all too familiar in the New Lodge. Most pubs in the area had been visited by Loyalist bombers at some stage.

A few weeks later, whilst grieving for Sharon and trying to comfort his little girl, Alan took her 'downtown'. There he met a young man from the Saltshaker who, over a burger in a café, expressed his sympathies but tried to offer some kind of justification, despite the terrible casualties, for the attempt to bomb the premises above the fish-shop. He spoke of the threat being posed by the Ulster Defence Association to the lives of ordinary Catholics and the common belief that UDA leaders were meeting on the Shankill to plan further killings of Catholics.

Baffled and distressed, Alan said 'You're brainwashed!', left the café with Zoe and walked away.

He did not go back to the 174 Trust for many years. [114]

Many years later, Henry Davis still recalls the 'lovely-looking girl' that Sharon once was. He remembers sitting in Alan and Sharon's house while she played the guitar and sang.[115]

Farewell to the Saltshaker

In 1994, the Provisional IRA declared a ceasefire, followed by the Irish National Liberation Army. A similar declaration was issued by the joint commands of the Loyalist paramilitaries, including spokesmen for the Ulster Defence Association and the Ulster Volunteer Force. Although these events did not stop all conflict, they reduced Northern Ireland's death-toll very considerably and led to a calmer, safer civic atmosphere, in which open political negotiations could begin, leading to the establishment by 1998 of a local power-sharing administration. Closer cross-border links in Ireland were then put in place. Cross-community agreement was also established that Irish unity could not be 'forced' on the Unionist people.

There was also agreement about prisoner releases, the creation of a new police force and a series of 'de-militarisation' measures by the British government, including a radical reduction of the army presence on the streets of Northern Ireland.[116]

For the 174 Trust, the mid-1990's also meant further change and challenge. In 1995, having survived through the 'Troubles', the Duncairn church amalgamated with the nearby St. Enoch's congregation and an opportunity emerged to move the 174 work into much larger premises in the old church buildings, including the capacious manse where Patton had lived since 1977. Under trust law, the premises had to be offered for sale to the highest bidder and in order to out-bid competition for the purchase of the site from secular and commercial sources, Patton and his committee had to obtain help from an influential businessman, who persuaded a bank to provide the necessary and substantial loan.[117]

But the mid-to-late 1990s were difficult times, despite the arrival of the ceasefires and the Belfast Agreement. One night, a group of young trouble-makers set fire to the contents of a skip which was lying in Duncairn Avenue and they subsequently attempted to throw burning debris at the church. The fire brigade and police were summoned and the church was saved from destruction.[118]

Kenny Groves, who had several years of connection to the trust, took on a key role in the transition process along with another expert in the logistics of Christian community work called Eddie McDowell. Kenny and Eddie could see that Christian evangelism as traditionally understood in Northern Ireland was less of an option, now that the Duncairn congregation had gone, along with its busy Evangelical clergyman. They knew too that the era of 'service provision', as typified by the ACE scheme, was coming to an end in Northern Ireland and that a 'community development' model must take its place, focused on enhancing the social capital and stimulating the economic initiative of the local community. Kenny tried to show the board that the new director must be someone who had the skills to go 'out there' and bring the community into the trust rather than trying to take the trust outwards on a mission to the community.

This would mean doing things thought impossible a few years ago, such as inviting a local Catholic cleric and a local Catholic lay representative onto the board.

Whilst re-thinking some of the 174 ethos, Kenny and the other board members recognised that the youth work would need revitalized, very possibly with the assistance of the Frontier Youth Trust, which had been a key presence at 174 for a number of years, through people like Maurice Kinkead and Joe Campbell. In due course a volunteer from England called Philip Hoppner would be installed in a house in Thorndale Avenue during the new dispensation described in part three of this book. He would liaise with the American church-worker, Doug Baker, who co-ordinated a scheme for sending over further volunteers from the USA to assist with the 174 youth clubs. The community development model which 174 would adopt was partly the result of creative thinking by FYT personnel at this period. [119]

Permanent change was underway. And saying farewell to the Saltshaker, the flats and the famous back-room was a sad affair for those who had worked there or benefited from the presence of the trust in their locality.

The church premises soon possessed an extension which became a cafeteria called the Manse Restaurant. The renovated church buildings were now named the 'Duncairn Complex' although they were under the management of a body still known as the '174 Trust'. For a short while, the ACE scheme moved back to the new, spacious premises, before ACE was finally ended by the government.

By this stage Patton - although he still headed up the 174 committee - had been recognized for his academic talents and was called in 1994 to the Chair of Old Testament Studies at Union Theological College in the university area of the city. In due course, he handed the chairmanship over to the community-oriented Baptist pastor, George Crory.

Patton, his wife Marlene and their five children were glad to make a new start. In truth, the time at the trust had often been frightening. When he was still single, Patton had once come back to find a drunk sleeping in his bed, after breaking into the manse. The elders of the church wanted him to move to a more secure location but he refused. At one stage a local graffiti artist had painted 'Vote Sinn Fein' on the church walls in bold letters, to indicate support for the IRA's political party at local election time. Fortunately, Sinn Fein's local representatives then ensured that the words were removed.

Far more terrifying were the stray bullets which became a hazard during sniper attacks. On one occasion, Marlene had come into Patton's study, only to find him kneeling on the floor, typing up a thesis. He told her it was a 'safety measure', as there had been a gunman active somewhere out beyond the window. The Taylors moved their children's beds away from the bedroom windows, as shattered panes occurred on a regular basis - not due to sectarian attacks but to general mayhem during riots in the surrounding streets or the shock-waves from bomb-blasts or random anti-social behaviour.

And on more than one occasion, the family had lain on the floor in the front room to avoid bullets during a gun battle.

On one other occasion, Patton had to intervene to prevent soldiers administering a lethal beating to a local lad in an entry near the church. The sense of stress for the Taylor family had been increased by isolation from the rest of the Presbyterian community in Belfast, who seemed oblivious to what the 174 project was trying to do and the risks that were undertaken on its behalf. Most Presbyterian ministers seemed to reside in the safety of the suburbs or the relative tranquility of the countryside.

However the loyalty of local people had generally been gained. Several generous acts of community support were particularly responsible for this, including help given on one night when soldiers ejected scores of residents from their houses in the Thorndale area, in order to search for IRA equipment after a 'bomb-scare.' Patton had opened up the church premises to accommodate his homeless neighbours.

He also went to court on a regular basis, testifying on behalf of local youths, behaviour which earned him a lot of New Lodge respect.[120] Nonetheless, there had been suspicion in certain quarters that this eccentric Protestant minister at Duncairn was in fact a 'special branch' man in the Royal Ulster Constabulary. One woman, whose husband was involved with the IRA, was heard to say that Patton had been carefully 'checked out', just to see if he was an 'agent'.[121] Such suspicions had certainly been aroused because of Patton's occasional visits to Girdwood barracks, where he took religious services for the troops.

It had occurred to him on more than one occasion that local people knew perfectly well that his sympathies were extended to the army as well as to themselves. Some soldiers on patrol took up residence in the church grounds one wintry night. Feeling sorry for them, he went to the local chip shop to buy them a fish supper each. Surprised by the size of the order, the lady behind the counter said –

'My goodness, you would think you were feeding the entire British Army!'

It may seem that Patton Taylor trod a thin line of varied allegiance during his New Lodge years.[122] However, in the eyes of one former Saltshaker regular, Patton was always seen as a man of the cloth whose job must entail being a go-between.

After all, a number of local Catholic priests also went in and out of Girdwood.[123]

Patton reckons he had a good relationship with Catholic clergy, who generally tolerated the presence of 174, admiring the social involvement but quietly warning young church-going Catholics like Jonny Owens not to succumb to the trust's more 'extravagant' religious enthusiasms. Patton had a closer bond with the Holy Family Catholic church on the Limestone Road than St Patrick's on Donegall Street. A small ecumenical group known as the 'Lamb of God' community (subsequently renamed the 'Shalom' community) lived and worked on the notorious interface at Duncairn Gardens and its members regularly brought Patton along to meet the Holy Family parish priest for discussions.

Patton was happy to keep up the links with the Catholic clergy on matters of common concern and he tried to make it clear that the trust was not focused on getting local people to switch allegiances. Nonetheless he explained that the 174 experiment had a very different ethos from that of mainstream Catholicism. And as a minister influenced by the 'reformed' faith, he argued that ecumenism should not stifle liberty of conscience. Any person ought to be able to convert from Catholicism to

Protestantism, if so convinced – or vice versa.[124]

However there is also evidence that people in the New Lodge community occasionally wondered if the 174 was an embryonic cult. Jonny's father certainly did. He worried that his son was being 'brainwashed', especially after opening one of his son's letters, which contained a message from Bill Fleming that congratulated Jonny on his 'conversion,' in the most euphoric of terms.[125]

Another great worry for Patton had been the financial balancing act involved in keeping the trust in existence. The covenant system which was employed committed a number of donors to five years of monetary support for 174 and this gave the 174 board a level of budgetary stability from year to year. However unexpected expenses led to sudden crises and Patton was then glad of help from men such as Dr Robert Caldwell, a local GP who was a co-founder and trustee of the 174 project and who on more than one occasion provided a substantial cheque when 'the cupboard was bare.'[126]

But now the directorship of the trust was officially vacant, ever since the resignation of Derek McCorkell. Philip McClean, as temporary leader, was doing his best to 'steer the ship' in the right direction.'

The environment which a new director would inherit was very different from that experienced by Mary Malanaphy in the early 1980s. The IRA's armed campaign had been replaced by community activism, conducted by ardent young Republicans belonging to the swiftly growing ranks of Sinn Fein. The economic recession of the early 1980's had been replaced by growth. However drug and alcohol abuse and gang warfare were now plaguing many parts of the city that were arguably suffering from a collective form of 'post-traumatic stress disorder'.

The New Labour government of 1997 was offering a 'New Deal' strategy for reducing unemployment and 'skilling' disadvantaged communities. And in the New Lodge area there were now several vibrant groups devoted to social and economic regeneration, such as the Ashton Centre, whose premises had been operating since the early 1990s.The Glenravel Local History project, superintended by Joe Baker, was doing a lot to sustain local pride and promote the area's heritage. However the wounds of the Troubles remained unhealed. Too many lives had been lost and too many hopes had been crushed for a renewal to swiftly and naturally occur.[128]

The new appointee to the '174' directorate was called to his post. His name was Bill Shaw and he would take the trust in the new direction that Kenny Groves had foreseen.

3

THE DUNCAIRN COMPLEX

Healing old wounds?

Bill had experienced Christian conversion in 1982 and a short time after this he heard about the 'Christian café' being run on the Antrim Road, so he called in one day to see what was happening. However there was little follow-up to this first visit as he was soon absorbed by training for the Presbyterian ministry.

Nowadays, Bill looks back on his 'early self' as a man with his 'theology all sorted out' and little appetite for experimentation. However when he became the assistant to a Presbyterian minister in a Loyalist working-class part of Belfast he soon discovered that the institutional church was doing little in the vicinity to build relationships with a community that had been damaged by the Troubles and by endemic poverty. Seeking to experiment with new methods of community engagement, he was told by one church leader:

'We don't do social gospel, we preach!'

Moving from the city to take charge of a congregation in the town of Craigavon, County Armagh, Bill was shocked to witness personal and community dysfunction in housing estates quite close to his church building, yet he could see that most Christians did not know how to intervene in such situations, other than to issue the usual, unheeded invitation to 'come to church'. Once again, 174 appeared in Bill's journey of faith, as he sought out Patton Taylor for advice on how to be a radical and practical Christian presence in an area of social need.

Old and inherited suspicions about Catholicism also vanished as Bill got to know local Catholic clerics and their parishioners. The post-ceasefire optimism of Northern Ireland was being disturbed throughout the second half of the 1990's by the annual confrontations which erupted at Drumcree, not far from Craigavon.[129] At this time, Bill felt an obligation to reassure his Catholic neighbours that he bore no ill-will towards them.

By 1998, he had decided to apply for the directorship of the 174 Trust, even though his experience of Republican communities such as the New Lodge was limited. On being offered the post, he headed back to Belfast to live.

Looking back to that early period, Bill reckons he still saw himself in fairly traditional mode. He was a self-styled 'missionary' to Catholic North Belfast, despite the new thinking that he had done about inter-church relations whilst in Craigavon. Residual wariness of the Catholic church surfaced when at an early prayer-meeting on 174 premises, a nun called Sister Carmel who lived in Thorndale Avenue made an appearance. However, the deep devotion manifested in her prayers soon convinced him of the authenticity of her faith. Bill reckons that this was God's way of 'reminding him' that He was already here and at work in the New Lodge, as He was everywhere, in various ways that he had been too blinkered to credit.

It was Bill Shaw's turn to get to know the community just as the other 174 directors had done.

He walked the streets. He met local people and invited them into the Duncairn buildings to see if the premises could be of use to them. He leafleted the entire complex of New Lodge flats, proposing events or clubs that the trust could host and which might benefit community life. He offered outings and sports to disaffected young people. He met local Catholic clergy and sisters and assured them that he was not in the business of 'sheep-stealing' Catholics from their 'fold'. Sister Carmel and Sister Gemma, who belonged to the Catholic order of the Little Sisters of the Assumption, also served the needs of the New Lodge from a house in Thorndale Avenue. At one stage a larger group of sisters had operated a refuge in this house for young single mothers. The two remaining nuns would become welcome visitors at the trust.

Bill felt liberated to experiment. Although he was, and still is an ordained Presbyterian minister, he was not officially answerable to a congregation, a local presbytery or the General Assembly of the Presbyterian church. He was also starting to recognize the true humanity of a community that during the 'Troubles' he had heard vilified as 'IRA scumbags'. It became very clear to him that God loved the people of New Lodge just as much as he loved any other citizens of Northern Ireland.

Bill brought locals increasingly into the Duncairn Complex. Numerous North Belfast people applied for vacant posts, in a process that was subject to Northern Irish Fair Employment legislation and transparent, open recruitment processes that were not mandatory when the 174 Trust began its work, many years before.

He invited the Community Festival to hold events in the church hall, including the 'New Lodge Talks Back' public debate. An Irish-medium school had its origins at the complex in 1999 and it swiftly began to thrive. It moved out to local Catholic primary school premises for a while but then found itself 'homeless' and was invited to return to the Trust. The Irish language nursery department still remains at Duncairn in 2010.

A boxing club which had been utilising a room in the complex was also encouraged to apply for funding and expand its work with local youths. By 2008, every available space in the church, manse and grounds was being used throughout day-time and night-time hours.

Bill also attempted to enter into community life in new ways. He joined the committee of the New Lodge Festival, became a chaplain to the nearby Cliftonville football club and undertook 'restorative justice' training so as to offer his services locally as a mediator in the field of offender-victim reconciliation. And in attempting to guide the trust towards a 'peace and reconciliation' agenda, he began to think of ways in which the Duncairn Complex could offer a safe space for all the traditions in North Belfast to find some common cultural ground.

In due course, he has sourced grant-aid to turn part of the Church into a centre for Northern Ireland's rich linguistic heritage. He has envisaged the 174 Trust as a place where the Irish Language and the Ulster Scots tongue could be freely spoken and celebrated, as well the languages of the new immigrants who were now making an appearance in Belfast.

Language has been seen as a badge of cultural difference in Northern Ireland's polarized society. Unionists often distrust the Irish language, seeing it as a 'political tool' for Nationalism. And advocacy of the Ulster Scots tongue has been seen by many sceptics as an artificial attempt to turn a dialect into a language in order to create a Unionist bulwark against 'Irishness'.

Yet Bill believes that in the safe space of the 174 Trust, local Unionists might learn that the Gaelic languages are an unthreatening part of their own 'British-Irish' inheritance and local Nationalists might also re-discover that many of the separatist heroes who fought in the United Irish Rebellion of 1798 were actually Presbyterians, motivated by a form of Republicanism that their descendants forsook.[130] Most of these men and women of 1798 spoke in a tongue that was arguably an authentic forerunner of what is now known as Ulster Scots.[131] Bill's hope is that the complexity and inter-relatedness of each community's cultural narrative will be more fully explored and enjoyed.

Already, the Duncairn premises have been utilized by the McCracken Summer School, which is an annual celebration of the Irish Language. Recently, 'Gallic' speakers from the deeply Protestant culture of Scotland's Outer Hebrides have attended the school and shown that a Celtic language and a Protestant identity can exist together.

In 2003, the infamous 'Holy Cross' dispute threatened to blow North Belfast apart. It centred on a Catholic primary school whose parents were taking their children to school by a route deemed to be intrusive on a small Protestant part of the area known as the Ardoyne.[132] As negotiations proceeded between the two sides in this confrontation, Ardoyne's Catholic community asked Bill Shaw to be a mediator in the discussions. He liaised with members of this community to hear their concerns and he chaired key negotiations at Belfast Castle.[133]

Bill has come under criticism from some community leaders in areas of Loyalist Belfast, who ask why the 174 Trust should focus on the New Lodge and not on vicinities such as the Shankill and Tiger's Bay, which possess bad conditions and possibly have a deeper sense of political abandonment. However, increasingly Bill has been involved in work within Loyalist communities such as Tiger's Bay and the Lower Shankill, alongside his commitment to the New Lodge.[134]

No-one here thinks they are better than anyone else

The trust's board members do not believe that their faith has been abandoned and they indicate that the trust is still rooted in 'the proclamation of the Kingdom of God through demonstrating Christ's values in action', which they stated on their website in 2009. But the board has been mainly preoccupied with handling practical affairs rather than theology. The 174 Trust's activities are conducted in buildings which need repairs, winter-time heating and public liability insurance. The paid staff members require their monthly salaries. Minibuses need maintained and refueled. Funding has come from a variety of sources such as the Department of Foreign Affairs in the Irish Republic, the International Fund for Ireland, the Community Relations Council and Belfast City Council. These funds could not have come if the trust had been pursuing anything other than an 'equal opportunities' agenda, in which Catholics and Protestants in the workforce operate together and no religious subversion or privilege could be perceived in the trust's make-up and strategies.[136]

It is unquestionable that the 174 Trust has now become woven into the very fabric of the community. Few workers at the trust have seen more during this recent period than Pat O'Neill, who has functioned as a caretaker and general organizer for the last decade. Pat talked with enthusiasm about his working life, when interviewed in 2008. He explained how was being paid to do 37 hours of work but that in reality he often worked for up to 60 hours. To come in on 'days off' was often a pleasure if he could contribute to the trust in any way. When he started the job, there were 9 local groups using the buildings. Now in 2008 there were 30 and there wasn't a space that he couldn't rent out.

However, as a caretaker he was all too aware of the effects of inner-city vandalism and of more organized kinds of theft. During one summer, 400 fine quality slates disappeared from the roof. Windows have been broken and arson has been attempted. £25,000 of damage was done when a 'joyrider' drove into the front of the church. More recently, valuable lead was stolen from the church roof during a spell of wet weather, resulting in a drastic problem with leaks. It is a testimony to the trust's public reputation that a builder repaired the damage anonymously and entirely without charge.

Asked why the trust works so well, Pat said that 'in this place, no-one thinks they are better than anyone else'. Everyone works hard but the mood is relaxed. If you are a visitor, you are usually welcomed with a cup of coffee and made to feel at home.[137]

Kate Clarke is not a paid worker at the trust but she has been connected to 174 for many years, as an advocate of Irish-medium education. Struggling to find a suitable venue in the New Lodge for an Irish Language classroom, she received an invitation from Bill Shaw to base the project temporarily in a 'portakabin' in the church grounds. So, in 1999, more than a dozen pupils of nursery age (up to 5 years) arrived at the trust, and the sound of little children speaking the Irish Language was heard on a daily basis in a former Belfast Presbyterian manse.

Before long, numbers grew and so plans were made to expand to primary age tuition (up to 11 years). Another temporary classroom was acquired and a room in the former manse was also used. An opportunity then arose for the school to move to less cramped facilities belonging to the 'Catholic Maintained' education sector. However this was a temporary move. The Catholic Council for Maintained Schools decided to close down the facilities and Kate's children and staff were 'out on the street', feeling distressed.

Once again, Bill offered the Duncairn Complex to Kate. For two more years, the children were accommodated at the trust, until the older pupils were guaranteed a spacious new venue at Lancaster Street, leaving the younger ones to stay in the temporary 'portakabin' facilities at 174.

When interviewed, Kate spoke of her warm memories of the time spent by the older boys and girls in the 'manse' before the final move. Bill called in each day to say a few newly-learnt words of Irish to the children who saw him as a friend and a mentor. She believes that without the 174 Trust, Irish-medium education in the New Lodge might have foundered. Her recent experiences have been in contrast to those of her early childhood, when she never dreamed of entering the grounds of the Presbyterian church, which was a place that Protestants went to on Sundays, a place that on a dark evening seemed to be full of strange 'bogeymen.'[138]

The Memory Tree

Caroline Foster has operated a very different education project at the Duncairn Complex. This is the North Belfast branch of 'Pathways', which is a service for young people in Northern Ireland whose behaviour is no longer tolerated by school authorities or who have excluded themselves from schooling, despite much discipline and counseling.

These young people can choose to attend a 'Pathways' course for one year, where they will experience a much more flexible but well-planned educational and therapeutic system run by tutors such as Caroline. She has worked with this small group of 'problem' teenagers on what is preventing them from getting an education, whether it be drug abuse, low self-esteem, anger management issues or a grim set of home circumstances.

Numeracy, literacy, social skills, information technology, first aid and art are among the things that Caroline has helped to deliver. There is group-work in order to encourage negotiation skills. Counseling is available to help the young people deal with difficulties. Some cannot get through the day without smoking cannabis. Some have watched a parent make a number of suicide attempts. Others exist in homes where the adult presence is weak and consequently they have had to achieve their own simulation of 'adulthood', much too soon.

For Caroline, there has been satisfaction in this challenging job:

'We see changes as they progress and become better when they are with us. And young people who used to be with us still come in for a chat. Some are proud to tell us that they've now qualified for a good job.'

When interviewed in 2008, she said that she regarded the 174 Trust as 'an amazing place.' She felt that the young people were 'in a community here,' within which they were not just tolerated but welcomed. They respected the venue and caused no problems. She said that the trust is in contrast to many other ecclesiastical premises which she has used in her work. She maintained that church groups too often proclaim they are 'interested in hosting youth work within the community' but then try to sift out the 'problem kids', scared that they will damage church property or smoke and swear or 'do drugs' on the premises and damage its furniture and its reputation.[139]

Sadly, the result of a young person's un-communicated personal distress may be an attempt at suicide. Here too, the trust helps local people who have been affected. One such man is Philip McTaggart from the Cliftonville Road, who lost his teenage son Pip to suicide in 2003. Philip decided to let his own heart-break lead him towards helping others. He founded the 'Pip's Project' to further his aims.

Philip became aware of an idea used in America for memorialisation of those who have lost their lives through suicide. This involves creating, in the local community, a Christmas Tree dedicated to all who have died in this tragic manner. The project is called the 'Memory Tree of Lights.' Relatives and friends who are mourning a loved one at this difficult time of year, are invited to place a memento on the branches and to speak about the person they miss.

Philip McTaggart and his friends wanted to bring this idea to Belfast. But where could they safely place such a tree? And in what venue might they hold a function after the ceremony, when refreshments could be served? Bill Shaw was the first chairman on the board of the Pip's Project. He suggested to Philip that the Memory Tree could be erected in the grounds of the Duncairn Church and that afterwards the Thomas Sinclair Hall would be opened, when tea and sandwiches could be provided.

That December, Philip and his colleagues decided on the 18th day of the month as a suitable date for the ceremony. Then they dug a hole in the soil and 'planted' a large Christmas Tree in the church grounds, nervously awaiting the 'big occasion'. That day, they put out chairs in the hall for 50 people, set out cups and saucers and prepared some sandwiches. It was a cold and bitter evening and soon the snow and sleet started to fall. But would anybody turn up?

Before long, 300 people had gathered in the grounds of the church, coming not just from North Belfast but from far and wide. Bill Shaw gave a short address, a local choir performed some music and Jim Weir from the Forum for Action on Substance Abuse, which was based on the Shankill Road, also sang a few songs. The guests were invited to place something on the Memory Tree in remembrance of their loved ones.

People went forward and decorated the branches with rings, cards, poetry, letters, necklaces and even locks of hair. Names of vanished loved ones were pinned to the tree. The coloured lights glowed in the wintry darkness but despite the sorrow of the occasion, Philip felt that a hard-won celebration of lost relatives and friends was going on. Amidst the gloom, he sensed a note of consolation. But it was still a bitter time for him as this was his first Christmas without his 'wee lad'.

In the warmth of the church hall, guests were invited to say what their loved ones meant to them. Afterwards, everyone mingled. Amongst the conversations in which Philip participated was one with a family who had lost someone as long ago as 1983. It was only now, within the walls of the 174 Trust, that they had found a chance to publicly celebrate the loved one who had been taken from them and to speak freely with others who shared the same deep pain.

The Memory Tree stayed in the Duncairn church grounds until January and no vandalism took place. No mementoes were stolen and no bulbs were smashed. A decision was made to replace the temporary and seasonal structure with a more permanent memorial.

Another simple ceremony then occurred at the planting of the second tree, which was a birch sapling. Philip, who comes from a Catholic background, joined a Protestant lady from the Shankill Road and they performed a dedication ceremony together. Then Bill spoke a few words to indicate his faith in God's love in the midst of all this pain. He then presented Philip and the 'Shankill lady' with a cross made from the leaves of the original tree, a cross that represents God's willingness, in Jesus, to share in the very worst of human suffering.

Philip McTaggart became a busy man as the Pip's Project soon had a number of 'satellites' all cross the north of Ireland. Every so often, on his travels, he would stop off at Duncairn Avenue and stand for a few moments, looking at the Memory Tree, thinking about his boy and remembering the events of Christmas, 2003.

When interviewed in 2008, he explained how when he goes to meet a family in his role as a counselor, the first thing that greets him at the door is a hug, irrespective of whether he is in Tiger's Bay or in the New Lodge. Ulster's ancient rivalries are largely irrelevant when suicide strikes and comfort is desperately sought.

Philip recalled how in the past, ecclesiastical attitudes to suicide were very harsh. The bodies of those who had died in this fashion were often excluded from burial in consecrated ground. Even now he says he knows of a case where, at a funeral of someone who had taken his own life, a close relative was forbidden to receive the sacraments because she was deemed to be in 'a state of sin' due to an extra-marital relationship.

For Philip McTaggart the 174 Trust has become sacred ground. The place is, as he says, 'a haven.' Its leader and staff are 'non-judgmental' and 'open'. Local people see the trust as a place that has been gifted to them. That night of 18th December 2003 was 'a saviour to many people'.[140]

The trust also acts as a 'haven' for the clients with 'special needs' who meet there on a weekly basis, under the guidance of Evelyn. Over twenty members attended the adults' group the author visited it in 2008. It was clear that the group members possessed a range of physical, mental or emotional difficulties. On the night of 15th May, 2008, they had all been brought by minibus from various parts of the north and west of the city, spanning cultural, religious and class divides.

Unfortunately not everyone was able to come that night. One man who normally attends had been suffering all day from painful fits. A 'Well-Being Centre' which operates in Duncairn Gardens, was conducting a free 'massage session'. A peaceful atmosphere was induced by soft, tranquil music on a CD player as the club-members received a gentle head-massage and then a full massage of the neck, shoulders, arms and hands. Mostly the sessions were conducted in silence but a couple of members 'opened up' and spoke freely – one lady talked about the increased pain she feels in her limbs and another girl described how she lives in a care home and greatly misses her dead parents.

A number of helpers were assisting Evelyn, including Rosaleen. Her boy has Downs' Syndrome and was attending the 174 Youth Club for children with special needs. Rosaleen explained how she enjoys the work with Evelyn. The summer trips to McDonald's or to the lough-shore at Newtownabbey are enjoyable for everyone. She explained how the club-members are always 'looking out for one another' and how no-one categorises anyone else as 'disabled.'

Inevitably, sickness and death make their appearance at the club. Not long before my visit, a woman called Berenice died at the age of 37, after kidney failure. But the mood at the club was positive, as it always is, especially when the members attempt something creative such as ceramics. One or two club-members are very independent, despite their difficulties. Sean cycles everywhere and also enjoys train-rides. He adores going to the circus. He has a remarkable gift for remembering dates and is an enthusiastic conversationalist.

On the might of 15th May, as the session concluded, the clamour grew for one particular lady to sing. She has been blind since she was seven years of age and lives alone with her guide dog. And so she sang, in a strong, well-trained contralto voice, surrounded by smiling, attentive faces:

'Oh Lord my God, when I in awesome wonder,
Consider all the works thy hands have made,
I see the stars, I hear the rolling thunder,
Thy power throughout the universe displayed,

Then sings my soul, my Saviour God to thee –
"How great thou art, how great thou art!"
The sings my soul, my Saviour God to thee –
"How great thou art, how great thou art!"' [141]

However, each week the trust also resounds to the more robust noise of an amateur boxing club. Since 1996, it has trained young men from the neighbourhood on the church premises in a special boxing ring. The organizers believe the club keeps young lads out of trouble and offers them focus and discipline. Some former members have gone on to be Olympic medalists and such famous boxers as Joe Frazier, Barry McGuigan and 'Hit-man' Hearns have all paid the club a visit. Pat McStravick, who is the key figure in running the club, comes from a local boxing family. His father was a prize fighter who boxed for money and had over 400 fights. Even on the day of his wedding he took part in a bout!

For the youngsters whom he trains, boxing is a door to the outside world. Some of the teenagers have never even travelled a few miles along the Antrim Road to such locations as the Bellevue Zoo. Taken to England for competitions, they get to stay in hotels and see a diversity of life that they would never otherwise experience. For Pat, the 174 Trust is always a great place to be. It is a venue that helps young men to develop a love of their chosen sport and charges a fair rent for use of the facilities.[142]

In the end, the New Lodge changed me

One of the legacies of 174 is the range of people who worked there, or who contributed to the various outreach activities that preceded the trust, and who have gone on to undertake further challenges.

Trevor Brock became a pastor in a country church in County Londonderry. In 2008 he was still working as a clergyman, in charge of the Great Victoria Street Baptist Church in the city centre. His predecessor, Roy McMullan, took up a job in the Irish Baptist College, on leaving Antrim Road and is now retired.[143] Patton Taylor became the Principal of Union Theological College, within Queens University, where Ireland's Presbyterian clergy are trained as well as students from a range of denominational backgrounds. He has received an MBE for his work as a padre with the Territorial Army in Afghanistan, an area of his ministry that ran alongside his roles as cleric, scholar and outreach worker in North Belfast.[144]

Mary Malanaphy now lives in Goucestershire, England, employed in an administrative role in the National Health Service. She rarely visits North Belfast these days but she retains fond memories of a period when she learnt so much about putting faith into action.[145] Her friend Heather Johnston moved to Dublin to work full-time for a Christian student organization. However she retained an interest in the trust throughout this period. Then she moved to Belfast with her husband, Joe Carey. In 2001, the Careys moved to a house in North Belfast, off the Upper Antrim Road. The opportunity to renew her relationship with 174 grew in all kinds of ways. Since 2002, she has been chairperson of the 174 board.

The long connection with 174 has been vital in her life. Working within a non-Protestant environment during the Saltshaker years enabled her to understand the religious sensibilities of the students she subsequently met in the mainly Catholic (or post-Catholic) Irish Republic. She refuses to be sentimental about the Saltshaker days and recalls the dangers that attended being a youth-worker there. She will never forget being thrown out of the door of the cafe onto the street, during one particularly rough altercation with an angry young man.[146] Henry Berry feels that his work in the Duncairn area gave him insights that would assist him when he moved to Dublin to work with the Child Evangelism Fellowship, south of the Irish border. Looking back, he considers his time on the Antrim Road to be a privileged one. And to his delight, he recognizes people he knew when he visits the area, although they are now adults with their own children.[147]

Laura Coulter moved from 174 to a City Council-run community centre in the Sandy Row, which is an ardently Loyalist area. She was struck by how similar the problems were in these 'opposed' communities. She looks back on the risks and freedoms of the 174 project and struggles with the baleful reluctance of the institutional church to engage fully with local communities and its desire to keep strict control over all its strategies and outcomes. Laura believes many Ulster Evangelicals are much too scared of risking 'corruption' by encountering 'difference'.

She says that exposure to the New Lodge also helped her realize why Republicans felt angry about the security forces. This gave her insights which helped in her work with the Parades Commission, a body which was set up to deal with conflicts between the 'Loyal Orders' and the Nationalist residents who oppose the routes taken by some Protestant marches. Subsequently she has also worked for the 'Peacemaking Board' of the Presbyterian Church and for the 'Healing through Remembering' Project.[148]

Tony Macaulay left the trust to work at the YMCA but returned in due course as a board member. Now he and Lesley run an organization known as 'Macaulay Associates' which is dedicated to consultancy work in many areas of social renewal, both here and overseas. He believes that the 174 story simply has to be told, in order to show that Protestant and Catholic communities were not hermetically sealed from one another during the Troubles and to allow the history of these years to be narrated 'from the ground up', in all its complexity. Tony knows that many people will hardly credit that the 174 Trust was allowed to thrive in an area of the city that the IRA was 'guarding.'

Tony notes that many young Saltshaker volunteers from that period went on to be key figures in Northern Ireland's civic life, working for peace, justice and reconciliation. In Tony's view, 174 taught all these people to think 'outside the box'. For him, a long process of spiritual evolution began. He came to feel that God was much bigger than Protestantism and more generous than in the strident format espoused by some Ulster believers.[149]

Lesley and Tony Macaulay now live in Portstewart, a town which overlooks the Atlantic Ocean. It is a long time since they lived in Clifton Park Avenue but Lesley still recalls the sight of Tony leaning out of their bedroom window into the darkness, to watch the rioting at the end of the street. The years they spent so closely connected to the trust were all-consuming ones. They needed to move on, especially when they began to think of raising a young family. In recent times, Tony has written a successful memoir, focusing on his life as a young 'paperboy' in West Belfast, prior to the years when he began taking an interest in the 174 Trust.

In her current work as a facilitator in the field of Community Relations, Lesley knows that the years spent working in North and West Belfast gave her valuable and painful experiences that she could never have learnt out of a textbook. She will never forget an occasion when a boy was on the run from the security forces and knocked on her door, seeking refuge. Lesley did not feel she should get involved and told him so. Scared and angry, he spat in her face and ran off. It was on occasions such as this, with spittle running down her cheeks, that she understood the tough realities of community work.[150]

These thoughts are echoed by Bill Fleming. Bill is back in Banbridge, working for the YMCA. He looks back at the Saltshaker experience and believes it was the foundation for everything else that he has done in the professional field. The work was unplanned and hazardous and the workers were without good professional training. Health and safety issues were rarely considered. However, the 174 years were the 'real deal'.

Bill says he learnt much about the duality of human nature, witnessing how the same people who were capable of violent fury could also exhibit sensitivity and genial kindness.[151]

The 174 Trust was influential in getting Bill, Tony and Lesley to think about 'community development theory' and to pursue practical, tested ways of lifting lives out of poverty and dysfunction rather than confining faith to a recitation of intercessory prayers for people with problems, or implying that God would solve all of those issues in a flash, when a person was converted.

When I spoke to him, Tony reflected on how:

'In the 1980s I came to the 174 Trust, determined to change the New Lodge - but in the end the New Lodge changed me.'[152]

This perspective on personal and social change is complemented by the comments of Kenny Groves, who helped the trust to make its big transition in the 1990s. Kenny believes that in the arena of youth work, change that happens in the workers is just as important as change that occurs in the clients. In fact Kenny often senses that the workers actually get more out of the process than those with whom they are interacting! He has seen workers from sheltered backgrounds, and with fairly narrow views, being positively transformed by exposure to the lives of young people whose everyday experience is one of deprivation, antagonism and risk.[153]

For Dave Maley, there are both pleasures and disappointments in looking back. He had come to Belfast, believing he would be part of a radical Christian community which would witness to a living faith by going beyond denominational boundaries, whilst living in a 'tough' urban area. That didn't happen, in his opinion. Many of the 174 volunteers would not move to the area to live, as had been planned. Or else they moved in and then moved away again. He understands why. It was very hard to bring up young children here. There were very many dangers.

He also became convinced that the trust was still, despite all denials, a front for the institutional Protestant church, which was seeking to rebuild its strength in North Belfast. Thus he thinks it was handicapped in its radical potential. He was increasingly 'turned off' by the pieties of Northern Irish Protestantism and he was also 'alone and scared' at times in a city he found very hard to understand.

However for several years he lived and worked at the 174 Trust and when he finally left he felt that it was a moral or spiritual failure of some kind. He was still still living in Belfast in 2009, working at St Mary's University College. He has continued to involve himself in community work and manifests particular enthusiasm for the spirituality of the Taize Community and what it can offer Northern Ireland. He has worked with Alan McBride on a weekly project which takes young boys from disadvantaged parts of Belfast to play sport together.

Rejecting the missiological dogma with which he once was imbued, Dave says that he sees true Christianity as rooted in radical behavior rather than dominated by pious words –

'My actions, my lifestyle choices, must validate and indeed precede anything I say....responding to someone's need is an act of worship.... faith that does not prompt you to make sacrifices for the sake of compassion is false piety.'[154]

When interviewed in 2008, Maurice Kinkead was living and working in East Belfast. For him the New Lodge experience had also been important. He had already seen when working in Protestant areas that youth work in tough situations enables workers to grasp what they look like to others. Young people in these communities respond with utter honesty to an outsider's faith, lifestyle, presumptions, personality and social class.

But 174 had also taught him to look beneath the surface and perceive much good in a community which many people despised for 'deliberately harbouring terrorism.' Maurice noted that many tough Republican activists had their values more carefully worked out, under difficult circumstances, than people who were sheltered in comfortable niches within his own 'faith-community.' In the New Lodge he was distressed at seeing some people doing violent things for the Republican cause. Yet many of these people lived sacrificially, practising altruism and promoting fairness amongst their own people. Above all, Maurice learnt that 'opening himself up' as a Christian through experimental community work, meant uncomfortably 'bumping into' paradoxes like that.

For Maurice, a 'living faith' is one which is in a constant state of interaction and modification.[155]

When Philip McClean was interviewed for this book, he was working as a consultant to charities which avail of his skills in order to begin successful fund-raising and to employ good business methods. He recalled the unique characters he got to know through the 174 Trust, such as 'Jimmy Joss' who lived at the Salvation Army Hostel and who came to the café for his 'grub.' Or there was Robert the chef who lived in a small apartment close by who was an expert on everything to do with the Islamic world, and who claimed - perhaps bizarrely but also truthfully - to have been involved in the early negotiations with Iran which eventually led to the high profile release of the Irish hostage Brian Keenan in Lebanon.

Nothing sticks in Philip's mind more than the community spirit which local people showed. He thinks that few middle-class church-goers ever manifest a similar attitude. He witnessed food being shared out each day among neighbours and he noticed how, when unemployment benefit arrived, the young men would share their money with their 'mates' on the unspoken presumption that they would get a share of other benefit cheques when they turned up.

Philip feels that local people did not react negatively to the conflicts that occurred in the 174 leadership or the human weaknesses that were often on view in people who were meant to be sanctified Christians. He thinks that a flawed 'humanness' in the workforce only made the trust all the more acceptable in the area. In one sense it placed the trust and the local community that it served on level terms.

Nothing is ever wasted

Having experienced the heartache of the Shankill Bomb in 1993, Alan McBride was determined not to let the experience shatter him. But his life was very tough. In the early months after the funeral, he went to the cemetery two or three times a week. He would later recall:

'Christmas morning was really painful. I knew the wee one would come through the door and she would be looking for Sharon and me, the delight on our faces. I felt angry with the IRA and with the Loyalists as well…'

A few weeks after the bomb, he had walked away from a 'Saltshaker regular' whom he met in a downtown café, unable to handle this young man's continued advocacy of militant Republicanism. But in due course, Alan was keen to rebuild the relationship and along with a few other mutual friends from the past, he met up with this young Republican and talked.

And in 2007, Alan joined Tony Macaulay, Dave Maley and one or two other former 174 volunteers in order to have a reunion with 'the lads' whom they had known during those Saltshaker days. Most of the invitees who met up on this 'Saltshaker Re-union Night' had become married men with children.

'You'se didn't make Christians of us after all!!'

- was one of the wry, amusing comments.

They went for a 'carry-out' in 'Manny's Chip Shop' as they had in the 1980's and chatted for a while in the Duncairn Complex. Then a few of them went to the Lansdowne Hotel to talk further, exchanging banter and anecdotes. Throughout the evening, Sharon's death and the killing of Billy Kane were hanging like half-acknowledged shadows over the proceedings.

As Alan looks further back to his early days as a committed Christian, he recalls attending a Bible Study on the Shankill Road, presided over by a man who asserted with 'scripture evidence' that the 'Church of Rome' was in fact the 'Antichrist.' Ordinary Catholics, according to this person, needed to be wrested from the grip of the Antichrist if they were not to burn collectively forever in the torments of Hell.

Alan feels that 174 taught him an important lesson. Taking 'Irish Catholics' out of the grip of the 'Antichrist' and making them into 'Ulster Protestants' would place them in a 'living hell', where they would have to turn their back on their family and culture and be totally reborn, though not in the sublime sense that Christ once advocated to Nicodemus. Alan could see that because of their deprivation, their demonisation by politicians and newspapers and their constant proximity to terrible violence, many working-class Catholics (and indeed working-class Protestants) had already been through a form of 'hell'.

Alan began to think that a Christian's job should include focusing on this social hell to which a difference could be made, right now. Society could be changed, so as to reduce violence and inequality. Christians could tackle a system that encourages intolerance and try to lift people out of the social depths into which they too often sink. As for the 'heaven' and 'hell' which the Christian church has generally believed to exist on the far side of the grave, Alan does not reject out of hand the idea of such destinies but he refuses to make easy or simplistic assumptions about such weighty matters and says that:

'who gets into each of these places will perhaps be more surprising than we think.'

(It must be acknowledged that such views would still be considered problematic by many Evangelicals in Ulster's Protestant community, for whom the utter certainty of heaven is one of the great joys of their spiritual life. And most Evangelicals feel that the clear and logical consequence of a life spent rejecting God is an eternity spent without Him. The choice, and the lines of demarcation, really are quite plain. For such believers, the path to heaven is as clearly signposted and followed as on the pages of Henry Berry's wordless book. That path is felt to be available, essential and relevant to New Lodge Catholics just as it is to citizens on the Shankill Road. It must also be noted that the expansion of the Christian Church has always involved the movement of the Gospel across cultural frontiers. The Church has almost always believed that finding a new identity beyond one's community of origin may be a costly but necessary part of the sacrifice required in a Christian commitment.)

Today Alan McBride is employed by an organization known as WAVE, which works with survivors of trauma inflicted by the 'Troubles'. He sees each day the lasting damage done to the survivors of violence. Alan does not think that everything about the 174 project was worthy of praise. He feels that the trust was set up and run in a rather random way. In particular, the volunteer workers were not looked after particularly well. Their accommodation was often poor and they were frequently expected to work themselves to the bone. However, despite such criticisms he has a gallery of memories from those pioneering days in North Belfast. One of his favourites is the sight of Dave Moser's house on Christmas morning, where local youngsters were lining up with their new bikes, to show 'big Dave,' who was their personal mentor. [156]

Kerry Nicholson, who worked at the Saltshaker in the early 1990s, is now employed by the Cedar Trust in South Belfast, which helps prepare people with disability for the workplace and the wider world, offering a chance to acquire a variety of skills and qualifications. He feels his time in the New Lodge was invaluable. It started broadening his horizons, showed him how extreme the Troubles often were and propelled him into social action, which he sees as a crucial part of Christian responsibility. [157]

A friend of Kerry's is Tonia Davidson who still resides in Seattle, from which she came to live in North Belfast two decades ago. Tonia has worked as a family therapist but has spent much more time recently with her three young daughters and her husband, Kory.[158]

Elsewhere in the USA, Dave Moser has worked as a Mennonite clergyman, having moved back to his native Indiana. After Beth's death, he developed a close relationship with an employee of the trust. They married and travelled to the States, to train at a college there, before returning to Belfast. Dave undertook an assistant pastorate in a Methodist church on the Springfield Road. But by 2001, his new marriage had come to an end and he returned for good to America. He met Ingrid, re-married and started a young family.

Dave Moser often reflects on his experience of Ireland, which in the end lasted nine years. He can still recall so many things from his Saltshaker days, including the sound of the children calling him across the street, to ask if he would like to have a go on their skateboards, or the cries of delight from those same children as they felt the spray of the

Glenarrif waterfalls touch their faces, on a trip to the Glens of Antrim.

He says of his time at the trust:

'I learned to laugh so hard I would cry. I learned to cry when there is pain, and I learned that the tears of pain and the tears of laughter come from the same place. I suppose one of the greatest lessons was learning to laugh when there is pain. When the tears of pain and the tears of laughter can come to the surface at the same time I believe healing can come to us. While there is pain and loss in life, nothing is ever wasted. There is always mercy waiting to bring a greater good from our brokenness.

I came back from Northern Ireland in June 2001 and in September, terrorists flew into the twin towers in New York. I first thought it ironic that I should have spent so many years living in a place "famous" for its struggle with civil unrest and with 'terrorism', only to return to the United States for a 'terrorist' attack on the World Trade Center that changed how Americans view themselves and the wider world.

In that moment, on 9/11, Americans became more fearful and in response to that fear they went to war in Afghanistan and Iraq. My country went to war, not to defeat any human enemy but to kill our deepest fears. And so, perhaps the greatest gift of all that I gained from my time in Northern Ireland is the simple lesson that we cannot "kill the fears within us" by trying to destroy or separate ourselves from the people that we believe to be the most deep personification of our fears. We can only overcome the deepest fears within us by learning to love ourselves and share that love with others. The work of overcoming fear with love is always something we do with God's help.

When I first went to the Saltshaker I was amazed at how courageous people were in facing those deepest fears, and being willing to overcome those fears in the pursuit of understanding and friendship. I hope that I am able to apply those lessons to the situation in which I now find myself, living in a country which in recent years has found itself overcome by fear.

The enemies we fear the most hold the keys to our redemption.' [159]

As Joe McGuigan looks back on those early years spent living in a city overcome by fear, he often wonders how he coped. On many nights he fell asleep to the sound of gunfire. He had watched violence come to his own door and he had seen friends 'blown away'. The Saltshaker was crucial in helping him to survive. He remembers 'deep' discussions into the night in the 'back room' that made him think more carefully about life and ponder his destiny. The Saltshaker youth-leaders showed him that he was worth taking seriously.

He understood that a way of life based on love was better than one based on despair. At one stage he committed himself to a daily faith and an Evangelical way of life but then he found that he just couldn't 'keep it'. He feels that becoming a seriously 'committed' Christian would have meant receiving a 'slagging off' from his 'mates' and it would have involved having to live out a new identity. It was too much to contemplate. However, the Saltshaker ethos still remains with him, especially the emphasis on doing good, living as if others mattered and trying to cross the divide that still disfigures this country. [160]

Two decades and more after those Saltshaker days, Joe has given help to Alan McBride and Dave Maley in a football project with young lads from various parts of the city. In 2009, the project involved a residential weekend and Joe came along. He got to know the young lads from places like Springhill and Westland. Many of them had never really conversed with a Catholic before. Joe then kept in contact with these young Protestants.

In fact, it may be argued that he was enacting a mirror image of the cross-community friendship that was shown to him at 174 Antrim Road, all those years ago. When Joe was interviewed, he spoke of plans to send some of these Loyalist lads on a trip abroad, courtesy of an organization that specialises in such projects, called Springboard.[161]

Working at Springboard in 2009 was Josey Grogan.

For Joe the reconnection with Alan has been especially important. After Sharon was killed in the Shankill bomb, the New Lodge 'lads' lost touch with him for many years. Now, some friendships have been resumed. Joe, Alan and Dave have been on cycle rides together into the Ulster countryside. In 2009, a small group of old acquaintances was meeting every few months and Joe had had a chance to show Alan that he and his 'mates' felt desperately sorry about what happened on that Saturday afternoon on the Shankill Road.

And did Joe perceive the 174 Trust as a Protestant enterprise? He is clear that he did not. He thought of the 174 workers as 'Christians' - neither Catholic nor Protestant but something altogether different.[162]

Joe's old acquaintance, Pat Grogan spent years in gaol and after his release he moved to South Belfast, where he has worked as a bricklayer. When interviewed in 2009, he was enjoying living in the calm, peaceful atmosphere of his part of the city. He was reading widely and was a regular in his local coffee-shop. He had travelled abroad, with rather more composure than on his first tentative stay with a Mennonite family in Ohio, many years before. He explained that he would love to have the consolations of faith but that he just can't 'believe'.

What Pat does hold in high regard is the genuineness of the Christian faith he witnessed at the Saltshaker, where the workers showed patience and astonishing courage.[163]

Jonny Owens has helped Alan and Dave with their voluntary sports project. He looks back at his Saltshaker days and feels grateful for the people who offered him help as he grew up in the middle of a war. However he reckons that the full implications of 'making a profession of faith' were not spelt out to him. He needed to be told more clearly that it involved a change of lifestyle. He needed a warning that 'conversion' would probably be perceived as a rejection of a Catholic identity. In one sense, Jonny has occasionally wondered if the lads in the Saltshaker weren't being subjected to a form of brainwashing at a vulnerable age and in very vulnerable circumstances. The 174 Trust offered warmth and hope and an intense sense of belonging which inevitably drew them towards a 'conversion' experience that they were utterly unable to sustain.[164]

When he was interviewed by the author in 2009, Jim Corry stated that he looks back with favour on the Saltshaker years and feels that he learnt a lot there. Admittedly he got sacked by John Evans from an ACE job as a painter and decorator but that was because he was a bad timekeeper. In recent years he has played music for a living and he recalls that he first learnt a few chords on the guitar from the Christian musicians among the volunteers at the café. He believes he met genuinely good people. That encounter with goodness has stayed with him as the years have gone by, even though he has left his experiment with Evangelical faith far behind.

He also feels, in an almost mystical way, that the place was 'protected' and 'safe' – a sanctuary amidst the gun-battles. He is unable to forget how in the aftermath of the killing of Billy Kane, Patton Taylor invited him into the manse and asked him how he was coping with the terrible news. That kind of thoughtfulness touched Jim.[165]

In recent times Henry Davis has been living in Glengormley, married to a Protestant girl he met at the Saltshaker. He is the father of two boys. During his time in gaol, he was visited by his friends in the 174 Trust. He also became very friendly with a prisoner from a Loyalist area of town and they played chess together and read books. Henry decided it was time to change his way of going, otherwise he would end up in prison once more or else lying forever in a graveyard. So on being released he decided to 'turn around'.

He regards the influence of the trust on his life as profound. He gives an example:

'I went into a KFC restaurant one day when I was Xmas shopping and I saw a chap come in who was clearly down on his luck and probably down-and-out. I heard some 'respectable-looking' women comment on his appearance and suggest that he oughtn't to be allowed into the café. I was furious. So I went up and bought a dinner and pulled a packet of cigarettes from my pocket and set the lot down in front of the man, saying

"Don't let those bastards put you out."

Would you believe that that man stopped me a long time after, in the town, and said

"do you remember me?"

He told me that he was the man I had once bought dinner for in the café and he wanted to thank me for the help. It had been one of the things that had given him the lift he needed at the time. He was now in touch with his family, off the drink and in better shape.'

Henry says this attitude was learnt in the Saltshaker.

In turn he wants to instill this attitude within his children. He wishes them to see how one small act can help change a person's life. But that they must not seek praise for doing it. And he wants them to realise that although North Belfast is still a troubled place, other parts of the world are very much worse. At Christmas he takes his boys abroad for a holiday. They have been to some fairly exotic places such as the Caribbean and Kenya. When they go to such locations, they enjoy the usual tourist sites but they also bring luxuries out of the hotels and give them to local people and make a point of visiting the slum areas which lie outside the tourist zone, where the inhabitants often live desperate and shortened lives. In Kenya, his sons discovered that a woman who worked in the hotel had seen her parents die because they could not afford medicine. The young lads realized that the price of that medicine was the money they would normally spend on a new game for their computer.

His interest in travel began when workers like John Frizell and Keith Spiers talked to him about their service abroad as missionaries. Henry began his own experience of travel through a youth service bursary, for which he applied while at the 174 Trust. It took him to the Scottish Highlands to learn new skills he would use as a youth worker at the Saltshaker. He also travelled to Merseyside with young people from the trust, to attend a Christian rock festival.

On two occasions during the 'Troubles', Henry's life was in particular danger. Once, a revolver protruded from a car window as he walked along his street. Then suddenly a police car appeared ahead and the would-be killers sped off, denied their prize of another dead Nationalist.

He recalls that the gun was shaking very badly and that this must have been the gunman's 'first hit'.

On another occasion, Henry was walking to work and he stopped to pick up an object which had fallen off a van. That object was an explosive device that had been attached to the vehicle. The bomb went off in his hand. When two nurses who had been passing by came to his aid, he had stopped breathing. They managed to resuscitate him and he was taken to hospital, bleeding and severely injured. He thinks that the attitudes which he first witnessed in the Saltshaker helped him to deal with the trauma and he says:

'I don't hate the ones that did that. I've changed. And after all, bitterness won't make my fingers grow back.'

But he is under no illusion about the 'bad' young lad that he once was, back in the era of the Saltshaker. He believes that the chaotic environment brought out that rebelliousness in him and taught him to enact a violent bravado, even though he was just a boy - and very scared inside. He tries to find various expressions for what the 174 Trust meant to him:

'a candle in the window in a dark street' or 'the calm eye of the storm' or 'a second home'.

He loved working in the café, once he had trained as a chef. He enjoyed introducing new dishes to the menu, such as lasagne, beef wellington, curry and healthy salads. He also understands that the trust had to change. The New Lodge is less beleaguered and Belfast is a better place to live. There are plenty of cafes and youth facilities around. The trust had to find a new role for itself and it had to evolve if it was going to survive.[166]

Another Saltshaker client and worker was Josey Grogan. Josey ended up in gaol once again, despite his period in the Christian ambience of the 174 community. This time he served a sentence of 4 ½ years. During that time, old friends like Derek McCorkell and Dave Maley kept visiting. Josey was embarrassed by the fact that these 'good' people had to go through humiliating searches on their way through the prison to meet him, under the eye of the prison guards. As he lay behind bars, Josey determined once more to alter his life upon his release from gaol. The memory of the years spent at the Saltshaker gave him a vision of how to go about that process of permanent change.

When he was let out of the prison in 1996, he set about doing community work with homeless people and he worked at a 'wet' hostel for alcoholics. He also began catching up on his education, mindful of the encouragement that the 174 Trust leaders had given him to fulfill his intellectual potential. He undertook a degree in History and Anthropology at Queens University and has subsequently obtained a Masters degree in Youth Work.

Josey has been working lately with 'at-risk' young people, including those who are in the 'care system', those who have been badly affected by alcohol, drugs and suicide and those who are classified by the legal system as 'young offenders'. He has trained other youth-workers and he has engaged in 'Outward Bound' projects which expose young people to the challenges and delights of the open countryside. Operating with a cross-border organization known as 'Springboard', he has often taken young people to other European nations where they can start to put their own troubles and the troubles of their native land into a broader perspective.

He has taken groups to Poland and Germany, where he is always struck by the massive impact made by a visit to the Nazi death camps. The bleak enormity of the Holocaust dwarfs all the quarrels and sorrows that young people have known in Northern Ireland and enables many of them to get a glimpse of how fortunate they actually are, compared with those millions of people who were slaughtered by the Nazis or who have become victims of other vicious dictators.

Josey has also witnessed the impact made by journeys to the Western Front in France and Belgium, where so many battles were fought during the Great War of 1914-1918. He recalls one 'hard' young lad with deep Republican views for whom wearing a poppy on Remembrance Day had been something that his 'Ulster Volunteer Force enemies' did. Then the boy went with Josey on a trip to the military graveyards of Flanders. Josey was relaxing in a café in Ypres before walking up to the Menin Gate for the daily act of remembrance there. Suddenly the young lad appeared before him, with his track-suit top exchanged for a jacket, in the lapel of which was a scarlet poppy. On being questioned by Josey about his change of attitude to this emblematic flower, the boy replied –

'I now see it for what it is ...'

However when interviewed in 2009, Josey was still perturbed by the aftermath of the Troubles. Despite the many good things that Henry Davis so rightly pointed out in the new Belfast, there is a widespread drug culture, there is youth disaffection and an alarming suicide rate and there are outbreaks of racism against the new waves of immigrants. Josey knows that growing up in the New Lodge can still be a hard journey. But looking back at the years he spent at the trust, he feels that the youth work which was done there was 'ahead of its time' and that he benefited in ways that are almost too great to measure. In his work with difficult and troubled young people he has been guided by a two-fold motto:

'never judge' and 'never give up.'[167]

Ricky Allen still keeps in touch with the Dutch friends who helped him so much as a boy and he visits Limburg quite regularly, with his wife and children. He thinks there would be immense benefit from getting young people from inner-city Belfast to move out of their tiny 'four street box' and see this wider world. In recent times Ricky has lived in Dunmurry and has also travelled the world. He feels that the war in the New Lodge and his childhood Catholicism have been left far behind. His paternal grandfather had been a Protestant and his mother was a Donegal Catholic, so there was a degree of complexity in the identity which he inherited but he could not have imagined as a young lad that he and his future wife would one day mingle with a suburban Church of Ireland congregation, as he has done in recent years or that his two children would be christened in this Protestant church.

Ricky hopes that attending the Sunday School will have given the children some kind of moral compass as they grow up in a complicated world and he has even found himself becoming less of a sceptic about religion, witnessing the excellent sense of community that this church provides. His young lad has been an 'anchor boy' – a member of the junior Boys' Brigade - and, according to Ricky, he has absolutely loved it.

Ricky still reflects on his own youth and in one sense, a trip to North Belfast still provokes nostalgia for his childhood and for his Thorndale home. But he does not miss the danger that often appeared out of nowhere in the New Lodge in those far-off days. He cannot forget how the much-feared Loyalist gunman Johnny Adair used to enter the area and casually engage in scouting activities. On one occasion, Adair jogged down Lepper Street with a copy of the Nationalist newspaper, the Irish News, sticking out of his back pocket while reconnoitering the district with intent to kill.

And when he drives through the New Lodge, Ricky can still point to familiar bullet-holes in the walls of buildings near the Duncairn Complex, marks that remain as a faint architectural legacy of the conflict.

Ricky also looks back on the 174 Trust and he suggests, with perceptive amusement, that the name is not inappropriate, because the organization meant 174 things to 174 different people! He was highly conscious that everyone who worked there had their own vision of what the trust was meant to be doing. He also knew that everyone who made use of the trust had their own way of incorporating 174 into their lives, of taking what benefits it offered, and of trying to make sense of this unique project that, so unexpectedly, had turned up in this intensely Republican Belfast neighbourhood, in the wake of a Protestant church community that had lost almost all of its parishioners.

But Ricky never votes. He is sceptical about politicians. He would like to see political tenure become like jury service – something a number of able citizens are obliged to undertake from time to time. The one thing that should debar someone from being a political representative is that they harbour an ambition to actually be a politician….[168]

Too dificult to keep?

Some Evangelical Protestant critics focus on the current lack of an explicit presentation of 'personal salvation' at 174, given that the trust is still led by an Evangelically minded cleric and supported in part by donations from Evangelical believers. These critics presumably want to see a continuation of what happened in the coffee bars and summer schemes of bygone years. However, those who make such criticisms may need to ponder a range of contributory factors, rather than blame any individual or clique for the trust's change of emphasis.

With the final departure of the Duncairn congregation and its minister in the mid-1990s, Evangelical Protestants clearly had less territorial 'right' to present their faith explicitly to a part of the city in which territoriality still desperately matters and in which Duncairn church members no longer belonged. And the trust project had not really succeeded in creating a confident, indigenous fellowship of local people who possessed an Evangelical commitment and who would have maintained a 'right' to witness to their neighbours. In fact, conversions had been few. And - as has been described in considerable detail - some of those who had made a commitment then turned their backs on it, as being 'too difficult to keep.'

(For Patton Taylor, there is still the hope, years later, that the Evangelical conversion which a number of New Lodge people experienced will prove to be an eternal change of heart. Although they may now feel unclear about what they once espoused, he hopes these converts may yet be restored to an Evangelical community that does not place them at odds with their culture. He feels they will finally be honoured by God for taking a stand for faith, in the most difficult of circumstances.) [169]

But many Evangelical Christians associated with the trust also changed their thinking, in part because of the interaction with the New

Lodge. Some came to feel that those cultural barriers which have existed since the 16th century are too great to be crossed by denominationally affiliated missionary work and that the post-Vatican Two Catholic church should maybe be trusted a little more to nurture a living faith in its people. This is consonant with changes of attitude in many Evangelicals towards Catholicism, worldwide and here in Ireland. In America, both of these denominational camps often came together for common moral purpose during the 1980s and 1890s, seeing secularism as a common enemy. In Ireland, 'old-style' Catholicism seemed well on the wane by the 1990s and many local Evangelicals felt less threatened.[170]

As a result, it was possible for those at the helm of the 174 Trust to consider that the only people with any serious chance of 'evangelizing' areas like the New Lodge were local Catholics who possessed a living faith, albeit one that was rooted in an unfamiliar sacramental tradition.

At the same time, the worst of the 'Troubles' were over and Republican areas such as the New Lodge were being versed in community development theory and practice, rooted in local self-empowerment, rather than imported assistance. The Saltshaker venture had of course recognised the need for its volunteers to live locally, but it had imported Evangelical workers to the New Lodge to provide the core of the organization. This went against the new 'good practice' in social policy which required truly indigenous and self-sustaining projects.

It should be remembered too, that for a long time the Saltshaker project was surviving on strenuous over-work from an at times exotic miscellany of young volunteers. It relied too on a very shaky budget. Some new way was needed to stabilize the 174 finances.

It is in these contexts that the decision to change the project should be seen. Generous new sources of grant-aid were available to the trust as the Peace Process 'kicked in' but only if it truly obeyed the rules of a modern community empowerment initiative, employing local people at every level and concentrating on building the social capital of the New Lodge in equal partnership with all relevant partners.

An ordinary kind of miracle

In his book about Northern Ireland, the Anglican cleric Nicholas Frayling has pleaded for 'healing spaces' where people can relate their memories of suffering, anger and survival, sharing testimonies of grief and hope, their love of the same places, their common human condition and their intricate and often conflicted histories.[171]

The gift of the Duncairn Complex to the New Lodge is the result of a journey of faith undertaken by many people who found themselves locked for better or worse within Northern Ireland's divided society. The long history of the vanished Presbyterian congregation at Duncairn is a key part of the story. The church travelled a long way from its foundation in 1862 to its 'closure' in the 1990s. In the 1860s the spire looked out on the open countryside beyond the New Lodge Road and across green fields to the new gaol on the Crumlin Road. The 20th century saw many changes. In 1914, 27 young men left the church to die in the trenches of the Western Front. Then in 1941, death rained down all around the church as the Luftwaffe bombed Belfast. In 1969, a longer local war than either of these two global conflicts tore North Belfast apart and the Duncairn congregation began to diminish.

One former worker at the Saltshaker has noticed how miraculous the survival of the 174 venture has been, given the local Protestant decline that it inherited, the turmoil-ridden society in which the trust was immersed, the disputes about direction and ethos in which its leaders engaged, the variety of personal failings sometimes exhibited by its workers and the enervating struggle to keep going on an often small budget.

This veteran worker paused at the end of a long interview before saying:

'You know, it was an ordinary kind of miracle.' [173]

Because of their vulnerable journeys, the congregations of the Presbyterian and Baptist churches on the Antrim Road, along with thousands of members of the local community and the workers and clients of the 174 Trust, have all bequeathed a 'healing space' for post-Troubles Belfast. In this space the stories which lie at the heart of all 'official histories' - and which often subvert them – can now be heard together.

As the Mennonite writer Jean Paul Lederach has pointed out:

'This is the deeper challenge of peace-building: how to reconstitute or re-story the narrative and thereby restore the people's place in history. When deep narrative is broken, we lose the capacity to find our place in this world. And we lose the capacity to find our way back to humanity.' [174]

Northern Ireland has been the location of deeply imposed stories and deeply self-imposed stories. It has been a place of damaged stories and of damage caused by stories. It has been a place where Evangelical believers who wish to tell the story of Christ's life and death for a troubled world have often felt speechless with shame, due to Ulster's compromised religious inheritance. It is in small 'healing spaces' such as the 174 Trust, that so many benign, awkward, dialogic stories were maintained throughout the 'Troubles.' It is a place where a number of severed narratives are now being resumed, where dubious stories can be meticulously questioned and where the gospel narrative may perhaps gain new clarity.

But outside the safety of such special 'healing spaces', the telling of both old and new stories of injustice, culpability and pain may possibly do little to promote the public good or benefit those individuals who feel most distressed. In particular, the habit of incessant agenda-led story-telling may lock communities or individual human beings into narrative loops, where characterization is constructed in terms of perpetration and victimhood and the plot features an unwinnable struggle between gain and loss.

In fact there comes a place and a time for untold stories.

Henry Davis carries the physical damage of the 'Troubles' with him, everywhere he goes. He sustained serious and lasting damage to an arm and a hand in the explosion that nearly killed him. His children often asked about these injuries when they were growing up and he told them that a shark had bitten him as he was swimming. When they are older, if they ask, he will tell them the truth. But when they were at a vulnerable age, he did not want to give his boys a motive to resent those who tried to destroy their father, or the community from which those would-be killers came. As he puts it:

'there are too many people still breast-feeding their children with reasons for hate.' [175]

Henry's comment is a reminder that because a story is true, that does not mean it should always be recited. Sometimes stories have to be set to one side. Sometimes gruesome reportage or the autobiography of grief need to merge into enchanted narratives that can facilitate growth, generate safety or promote healing. At some stage, old sorrows, rivalries, facts and furies – and the age-old templates of identity that they conjure up - have to fade away so as to make room for the future and to prevent a troubled past from continuing to occur in generation after generation.

Ricky Allen's views are relevant:

He has worked with 'broken' or troubled homes for the Dr Barnardo's project and this has involved Family Group Conferencing. It gives him a model for thinking about progress within the much bigger, troubled family that exists in the north of Ireland. In his interventions, Ricky often asks his clients to listen to one another's stories and try to see one another's point of view. The issues of blame and injustice are discussed and they are invariably rooted in the past. But then, after the stories have been heard, everyone has to start 'moving on'. What has been done can never be undone. But it must be left behind. Otherwise a bad past ends up creating a bad future.

In that way, no-one heals.[176]

Endnotes

1 The website www.thenewlodge.com has offered a survey of the area, past and present.

2 For a brief summary of Sinclair's life, see www.ulsterscotsagency.com/siteFiles/resources/sinclair.pdf, accessed June 2009

3 A short account of the civil strife in the early 1920s in Belfast is offered in Jonathan Bardon, *Belfast – an illustrated history* (Belfast, 1987) p. 188-203

4 Local man Joe Baker is an authority on community history and founded the Glenravel Local History Project which, among other things, records the stories of the New Lodge.

5 Among many books on the IRA is Richard English, *Armed Struggle – the history of the IRA* (London, 2003) On the subject of the INLA there is Jack Holland and Henry McDonald, *INLA – deadly divisions* (Dublin, 1994)

6 The lyrics of the song from which this verse comes were accessed at www.geocities.com/rollofhonour32/m.html, on 20/5/09

7 Among several book which give an insight into the hunger-strikes is Denis O'Hearn, *Bobby Sands – nothing but an unfinished song* (London, 2006)

8 D. McKittrick et al, *Lost Lives* (Edinburgh 1999) p. 859-862

9 Interview with Dermott McMorran, December 2009

10 Interviews with Trevor Brock and Roy McMullan, April 2008 and April 2009

11 Interview with Patton Taylor, May 2009

12 Interview with Ricky Allen, June 2009

13 Interviews with Patton Taylor, May 2008, May 2009

14 Interview with Trevor Brock, April 2008

15 Interviews with Patton Taylor and Henry Berry, May 2008, May 2009

16 Patton Taylor, 'The 174 Story' in Michael Eastman and Steve Latham, *Urban Church* (London, 2004) p. 97-100

17 Interview with Patton Taylor, May 2008, May 2009

18 Interview with Mary Malanaphy, January 2009

19 Interviews with Heather Carey, April 2008, January 2009

20 Interview with Heather Carey, April 2008

21 Interview with Pat O'Neill, May 2009

22 Interview with Heather Carey, April 2008, January 2009

23 Interview with Lois Balmer, January 2009

24 Interview with Joe McGuigan, March 2009

25 Interview with Laura Coulter, April 2008

26 The content of Interviews with several former Saltshaker clients, all of whom who are mentioned in this book, distinctly confirms Laura's opinion.

27 Interviews with most 174 volunteers confirm the regular existence and importance of these meetings.

28 Interview with Mary Malanaphy, April 2008

29 See the article 'Playing the Belfast Game' at www.britains-smallwars.com/ni/ken3.html accessed 10/2/09

30 Almost all the interviewees for this book, who were local residents within the New Lodge during the 'Troubles', share this common memory.

31 Interview with Joe McGuigan, March 2009

32 Interview with Tony Macaulay, April 2008

33 A website specifically dedicated to the memory of those who died and to further pursuit of the complete truth about the bombing may be found at www.themcgurksbarmassacre.com

34 Interview with Lesley Macaulay, March, 2009

35 Interviews with Dave Maley, April 2008 and March–May, 2009

36 Interview with Ricky Allen, June 2009

37 Interview with Alan McBride, April 2008 and May 2009

38 Interview with Jim Corry, April 2009

39 Interview with Alan McBride, April 2008 and May, 2009

40 Interview with Henry Davis, April 2009

41 Interview with Joe Baker, April 2009

42 Interview with 'Sean', March 2009

43 Interview with Jonny Owens, April 2009

44 This verdict came across strongly in interviews with several 174 Trust clients.

45 Interview with Jonny Owens, April 2009

46 Interview with Henry Davis, April 2009

47 Interview with Pat Grogan, May 2009

48 Interview with Maurice Kinkead, April 2008

49 Interview with Kenny Groves, May 2009

50 Memories of the Christmas 'food-run' were particularly vivid during a re-union event for 174 volunteers, held at the trust in January 2009

51 Interview with Henry Davis, April 2009

52 These stories were narrated during the January 2009 re-union at the trust.

53 Interview with Maurice Kinkead, April 2008

54 Interview with Lesley Macaulay, March 2009

55 Dave Moser's story has been brought together from an array of letters and diaries which he kept during this period of his life and also from later correspondence with the author, during September 2008 – January 2009

56 Interview with Pat Grogan, May 2009

57 David Moser archive

58 Interview with Patton Taylor, May 2009

59 David Moser archive

60 Interview with Josey Grogan, March, 2009

61 Correspondence with Chris Rogers, February 2009

62 Interview with Mary Malanaphy, January 2009

63 John Evans's career with the trust is briefly described in the personal archive of David Moser

64 Interview with Deena Nimick, April 2008

65 Interview with Bill Fleming, May 2009

66 For more details on this political process see E. Mallie and D. McKittrick, *Endgame in Ireland* (London, 2001)

67 David Moser archive

68 Interview with Joe McGuigan, March 2009

69 David Moser archive.

70 Interview with Pat Grogan, May 2009

71 Interview with Henry Davis, April 2009

72 Interview with Jonny Owens, April 2009

73 For details of both Kane family killings see www.themcgurksbarmassacre.com, accessed 20/11/08

74 Interview with Joe McGuigan, March 2009

75 Interview with Pat Grogan, May 2009

76 David Moser archive

77 Interview with Bill Fleming, May 2009

78 Interview with Pat Grogan, May 2009

79 Interview with Jim Corry, April 2009

80 David Moser archive

81 Interview with Henry Davis, April 2009

82 Interview with Lesley Macaulay, April 2009

83 David Moser archive

84 David Moser archive

85 McKittrick, p. 1112-1124

86 David Moser archive

87 Interview with Patton Taylor, May 2009

88 Interview with Tony Macaulay, April 2008

89 Interview with Philip McClean, March 2009

90 This anecdote surfaced during a re-union at the trust in January 2009

91 Correspondence with Louise van der Linde, January 2009

92 A couple of former 174 regulars have referred to the growing drug habit

93 David Moser archive

94 David Moser archive

95 Interview with Patton Taylor, May 2009

96 David Moser archive

97 Interview with Pat Grogan, May 2009

98 David Moser archive

99 Interview with Bill Fleming, May 2009

100 David Moser archive

101 From Alice Milligan's poem, Mountain Shapes, published in *Two Poems* (Dublin, 1943)

102 Interview with Kerry Nicholson, November 2008

103 For information about the 'raid' on 218 Cliftonville Road, the author is indebted to Dave Maley.

104 Interview with Kerry Nicholson, November 2008

105 A concise record of the Irish Famine is to be found in Ruan O'Donnell *Pocket History of the Irish Famine* (Dublin, 2008)

106 Interview with Ricky Allen, June 2009

107 Interview with Philip McClean, February 2009

108 Interview with Josey Grogan, May 2009

109 For access to extant recordings of these songs, the author is indebted to Dave Maley.

110 This written account of Tonia Davidson's experiences was given to the author in November 2008

111 David Moser archive

112 The above details about the bomb and Alan McBride's experiences and comments are found at www.iraatrocities.fsnt.co.uk/shankill.htm accessed 1/6/2009

113 Interview with Henry Davis, April 2009

114 Interview with Alan McBride, May 2009

115 Interview with Henry Davis, April 2009

116 Or further details see the updated version of Deaglan de Breadun's book *The Far Side of Revenge* (Cork, 2008)

117 Interview with Patton Taylor, May 2008

118 Interview with Ricky Allen, June 2009

119 Interview with Kenny Groves, May 2009

120 Interviews with Patton Taylor, May 2008, May 2009 and also several contributions made to a group discussion at a 174 reunion held in January 2009

121 This story was delivered in confidence by a friend of the trust.

122 Interviews with Patton Taylor, May 2008, May 2009

123 Interview with Jonny Owens, April 2009

124 Interview with Patton Taylor, May 2009

125 Interview with Jonny Owens, April 2009

126 Interview with Patton Taylor, May 2009

127 For more details see www.ashtoncentre.com

128 For more details see www.glenravel.com

129 For further details see Chris Ryder and Vincent Kearney *Drumcree – the Orange Order's last stand(* London, 2001)

130 Interview with Bill Shaw, May 2008

131 An introduction to the Presbyterian experience of the 1798 rebellion may be found in A.T.Q. Stewart *The Summer Soldiers (Belfast, 1998)*

132 Anne Cadwallader , *Holy Cross – the untold story* (Belfast, 2005)

133 Interview with Bill Shaw, May 2008

134 Recent working-class Loyalist issues have been studied in Philip Orr, *New Loyalties – Christian Faith and the Protestant working-class (* Belfast, 2008)

135 www.174trust.org/v3/index.php , accessed on 3/3/09

136 Interview with Heather Carey, June 2009

137 Interview with Pat O'Neill, April 2009

138 Interview with Kate Clarke, May 2008

139 Interview with Caroline Foster, May 2008

140 Interview with Philip McTaggart, June 2008

141 Visit to the 174 Trust by the author , May 2008

142 Interview with Pat McStravick, June 2008

143 Interview with Trevor Brock, April 2009

144 Interviews with Patton Taylor, April 2008 and May 2009

145 Interview with Mary Malanaphy, January 2009

146 Interview with Heather Carey, April 2008

147 Interview with Henry Berry, March 2009

148 Interview with Laura Coulter, April 2008

149 Interview with Tony Macaulay, April 2008

150 Interview with Lesley Macaulay, March 2009

151 Interview with Bill Fleming, May 2009

152 Interview with Tony Macaulay, April 2008

153 Interview with Kenny Groves, May 2009

154 Interviews and correspondence with Dave Maley, April 2008 to May 2009

155 Interview with Maurice Kinkead, April 2008

156 Interview with Alan McBride, April 2008 and May 2009

157 Interview with Kerry Nicholson, November 2008

158 Correspondence with Tonia Davidson, December 2008 – January 2009

159 David Moser archive

160 Interview with Joe McGuigan, March 2009

161 Interview with Alan McBride, May 2009

162 Interview with Joe McGuigan, March 2009

163 Interview with Pat Grogan, May 2009

164 Interview with Jonny Owens, April 2009

165 Interview with Jim Corry, April 2009

166 Interview with Henry Davis, April 2009

167 Interview with Josey Grogan, May 2009

168 Interview with Ricky Allen, June 2009

169 Interview with Patton Taylor, May 2009

170 A good example of a Protestant- Catholic encounter is the Clonard-Fitzroy group which has built a relationship of a sustained kind between an Evangelical Protestant and a Catholic congregation over the past three decades

171 The concept of healing spaces is developed in Nicholas Frayling, *Pardon and Peace* (London,1995)

172 Duncairn Presbyterian Church centenary booklet, 1962 ; a copy is held at the Glenravel historical project

173 Comment made under conditions of anonymity.

174 Jean Paul Lederach, *The Moral Imagination* (Oxford, 2005) p 146-147

175 Interview with Henry Davis, April 2009

176 Interview with Ricky Allen, June 2009